SILENCING CHINESE MEDIA

SILENCING CHINESE MEDIA

The Southern Weekly *Protests and the Fate of Civil Society in Xi Jinping's China*

Guan Jun

Translated by Kevin Carrico

ROWMAN & LITTLEFIELD
Lanham • Boulder • New York • London

Published by Rowman & Littlefield
An imprint of The Rowman & Littlefield Publishing Group, Inc.
4501 Forbes Boulevard, Suite 200, Lanham, Maryland 20706
https://rowman.com

6 Tinworth Street, London SE11 5AL, United Kingdom

British Library Cataloguing in Publication Information Available

Library of Congress Cataloging-in-Publication Data
Names: Guan, Jun, (Journalist) author. | Carrico, Kevin, translator.
Title: Silencing Chinese media : the "Southern Weekly" protests and the fate of
    civil society in Xi Jinping's China / Guan Jun ; translated by Kevin Carrico.
Description: Lanham : Rowman & Littlefield, 2020. | Includes index.
Identifiers: LCCN 2020002698 (print) | LCCN 2020002699 (ebook) | ISBN
    9781538142264 (cloth) | ISBN 9781538142271 (paperback) | ISBN
    9781538142288 (epub)
Subjects: LCSH: Nan fang zhou mo. | Press and politics—China—History—
    21st century. | Freedom of the press—China—History—21st century. |
    Censorship—China—History—21st century. | Newspaper publishing—Po-
    litical aspects—China. | Guan, Jun, (Journalist). | Journalists—China—
    Guangzhou—Biography.
Classification: LCC PN5369.G833 N365 2020 (print) | LCC PN5369.G833
    (ebook) | DDC 302.23/10951—dc23
LC record available at https://lccn.loc.gov/2020002698
LC ebook record available at https://lccn.loc.gov/2020002699

∞ ™ The paper used in this publication meets the minimum requirements of
American National Standard for Information Sciences Permanence of Paper
for Printed Library Materials, ANSI/NISO Z39.48-1992.

CONTENTS

not at all diminish its importance as a stand for a whole range of ideas celebrated and put into practice by the journalists involved—ideas about journalistic professionalism, public interest, the need for fact-based reporting, and so on—that many of us outside China would recognize as being akin to our own notions about the role of the media and the need for press freedom.

The story that follows provides a rare glimpse into the sometimes-baffling substance of actions and discussions within *Southern Weekly* as the protests continued outside the gates and online. Written by Guan Jun, a former journalist at *Southern Weekly* who at the time was no longer working at the paper but maintained a close connection with staff there, it is based on interviews with those involved, as well as access to firsthand materials (such as chat records) and other sources. Readers may think of it as an in-depth work of journalism in which a seasoned Chinese reporter turns the skills of his profession on an important story about that profession in the larger context of Chinese society and politics. In this sense, this book is in some ways an extension of the professional spirit long embodied, for many, in *Southern Weekly*.

What do those professional values mean? Our hope is that such questions might be answered, in whole or in part, by the story itself as one form of documentation of what happened in Guangzhou in January 2013. But we hope to offer the reader in the remainder of this brief introduction some sense of what *Southern Weekly* has meant for China since its launch in the 1980s, and why so many, not least Chinese journalists, felt that the stakes were so high.

"BORN IN 1984"

Southern Weekly (*Nanfang Zhoumo*) has long been regarded as one of the most influential and symbolic news media in contemporary China, and it was once considered "a publication with the highest credibility among the general public" and "the only paper with a soul."[8] It has produced numerous pieces of quality investigative journalism and published articles that express diverse opinions in a restricted political environment. It is perhaps the best case through which we can examine the changing landscape of journalism in China, and more generally, it also glasnost from below as China's society becomes more defiant and willing to challenge the Party's authority. But this means if the newly installed leaders want to maintain any credibility, they will soon be forced to take a stand on the most divisive and dangerous issue in China—political reform."[6]

The stakes, clearly, were high. But amid the observation and speculation, some of the most critical voices were absent. Most importantly, no one had yet heard from the *Southern Weekly* reporters and editors directly in the path of the storm. Days earlier, a group of prominent former journalists from the newspaper, including Qian Gang, the founder and codirector of the China Media Project, had spoken out in an open letter supporting *Southern Weekly* staff and sharply criticizing the actions of Guangdong's propaganda chief, Tuo Zhen, who was accused not just of intruding in an unprecedented manner on independent editorial decisions at the paper, but of directly introducing a number of foolish and embarrassing factual blunders—what the letter deemed "numerous errors and accidents"—into the highly celebrated New Year's edition, long seen as having an important role in setting the professional tone for the year. "We are media professionals who formerly worked at *Southern Weekly*, and we must voice our shared position on the recent '2013 New Year's greeting' incident at the newspaper," the former staffers wrote. "We feel that what has unfolded over the past two days is a matter of extreme seriousness."[7]

Still, these former editors and reporters, while in close contact with *Southern Weekly* staffers, were not directly involved in events as they unfolded, and they too were unclear about many of the details of exactly what had happened to prompt the strike action. The chief reason for this lack of clarity was the chaotic and constantly shifting nature of the strategic game unfolding inside the offices of the Nanfang Daily Group. Watching events from the outside, international media correctly observed the important role social media played in rallying support for the embattled newspaper. But they had no idea just how fractious the internal discussions had already become within the private chat groups *Southern Weekly* staffers used to suggest courses of action, communicate strategy, and unburden their emotions. The incident was not, as international reporting sometimes made it seem, an act of simple heroics, a principled stand on the hallowed ground of press freedom in the face of a Goliath system of press censorship. To say so, however, does

The government responded by censoring key terms online—not only words of obvious sensitivity such as "press freedom" and "freedom of expression," but also simple words with indirect associations with the protests like "Guangzhou Avenue," the address of the newspaper group, and even general references to "the south."[4]

For those watching from the outside, what came to be called the *"Southern Weekly* incident" seemed at the time to be an inflection point. Open protests calling for freedom of the press had not happened in China, certainly not on this scale, in nearly a quarter century—not since the crushing of pro-democracy demonstrations in 1989. Here, they were happening right outside the gates of the Nanfang Media Group, publisher of both the *Nanfang Daily,* the official "mouthpiece" of the Chinese Communist Party (CCP) in China's prosperous southern province of Guangdong, and of the newspaper inspiring the protests, the more freewheeling *Southern Weekly.*

Since its launch in the 1980s, *Southern Weekly* had become symbolic for many of the pro-reform spirit in China, and the ethos of openness and truthfulness so crucial, in the eyes of many, to sustaining reform. The protests were unfolding, moreover, just a few months after the Party had sworn in a new general secretary, Xi Jinping, at the Eighteenth National Congress of the CCP in November 2012. What kind of top leader was Xi Jinping? Was he a reformer who might seize on the opportunity afforded by the public outcry over press censorship, affirming the crucial role played by *Southern Weekly* as a reform-minded newspaper? Or was he a hardliner, sure to regard the hue and cry in Guangzhou as a brazen affront to his power and position and that of the Party?

On January 7, Victoria Nuland, a spokesperson for the US Department of State, weighed in on the event during her daily press briefing: "Well, as you know, we have long defended and supported the right of media freedom, both for Chinese journalists and for international journalists operating in China," she said. "It is, of course, interesting that we now have Chinese who are strongly taking up their right for free speech, and we hope the government's taking notice."[5] Writing in the *Wall Street Journal,* Minxin Pei, a professor of government at Claremont McKenna College, characterized the incident as a major test for China's new leadership, and a sign of an opening society that was now more resistant to curbs on freedom: "The incident shows the promise of

INTRODUCTION

The Rise and Fall of *Southern Weekly* and the Changing Landscape of Journalism in China: A Pivotal Event

David Bandurski and Fang Kecheng

On January 7, 2013, as hundreds of protestors gathered outside the headquarters of a major newspaper group in China's southern city of Guangzhou, foreign journalists dispatched to the scene might be forgiven for reducing a complex story to its barest essentials. The heart of this story was, to all appearances, "a battle over media censorship"—as the *New York Times* reported in an article that bore the headline "Protest Grows over Censoring of China Paper."[1] Under the watchful eye of police and security who seemed powerless to act, demonstrators massing along Guangzhou Avenue hoisted posters bearing messages such as "Resisting censorship of the news; give me back my freedom of expression," and "Abolish controls on newspapers; give me back my press freedom." Television footage, broadcast on CNN and other global networks, showed Chinese stepping up to the gates of the newspaper headquarters and laying down white and yellow chrysanthemums, traditional flowers of mourning, as they might before the grave of a beloved family member.[2] Online too, Chinese rallied to the cause—for, again, that is exactly what it seemed. Posting to her millions of fans on the popular Weibo social media platform, Chinese actress Yao Chen invoked the words of the Soviet-era dissident writer Aleksandr Solzhenitsyn: "One word of truth outweighs the whole world," she wrote.[3]

reflects the achievements and limitations of China's reform since the late 1970s.

Southern Weekly was launched on February 11, 1984, and over the next decade progressively transformed itself from a newspaper focused on entertainment, culture, and economics to a more serious publication by the middle of the 1990s, with a special section dedicated to more investigative stories. To mark the occasion of its twenty-fifth anniversary in 2009, it published an editorial called "Born in 1984." Although the piece made no explicit reference to George Orwell's novel on totalitarianism, acute readers could not escape the message coded into the headline. Sure, the newspaper had gained a reputation for pushing the envelope, fighting for whatever space it could—and in nine months' time it would be chosen by the Obama administration for an exclusive interview with the president during his visit to China.[9] But *Southern Weekly* was nevertheless a newspaper born and raised in a country in which the ruling Communist Party allowed only very limited press freedom.

China is not the Oceania of Orwell's *Nineteen Eighty-Four*. Though decidedly a totalitarian state before the death in 1976 of Mao Zedong, who had drawn from the Leninist propaganda model to construct a media system that served as the mouthpiece of the Party, and of himself personally, China in the reform period was a country in transformation. The economic reform policies pursued in the late 1970s, along with the recognition that Mao's total domination of the media had contributed to a "falsehood, exaggeration and emptiness" that exacerbated tragic missteps,[10] brought the reform and commercialization of the media sector from the early 1980s onward. *Southern Weekly* was one among thousands of media outlets launched in China in the 1980s, a process that accelerated in the 1990s.

Though never liberated from the yoke of Party control, these media enjoyed a certain degree of latitude, in part because they responded to the growing demand for information from a rapidly changing and developing society. Based in Guangdong province, where China's economic reforms first got under way, *Southern Weekly* is a subsidiary publication of the party newspaper *Nanfang Daily* (*Southern Daily*). It has the same ownership structure as *Nanfang Daily*—100 percent owned by the state—but its business model is completely different. While party newspapers are funded by the state and mainly distributed in the offices of the government and state-owned enterprises, commercialized news-papers (or "market-oriented newspapers") like *Southern Weekly* must rely on advertising revenue and retail revenue from newsstands. They are given more autonomy and freedom in terms of content—and they must produce non-propaganda content in order to attract readers and advertisers.

This structural change laid the foundation for the emergence of better-quality journalism in China as journalists and editors increasingly professionalized and sought to distinguish their work, for commercial reasons as much as idealistic ones. Journalists at *Southern Weekly* began experimenting with different types of content, beginning first with entertainment and celebrity news, and later investing in more in-depth and current affairs content that could both appeal to readers and fulfill their professional aspirations. They found a formula for success in two types of content in particular. The first was investigative journalism, exposing cases of corruption, social injustice, and other scandals. The second was the opinion piece, which could introduce more diverse perspectives on key issues, often taking a critical stance against Party and government power.

Make no mistake—the censorship system was never removed, and never particularly relaxed. Because *Southern Weekly* and other commercialized media outlets were still embedded within the party-press system, as subsidiaries of official flagship publications they had to follow marching orders and be cautious about what they published. But there were also formal factors that allowed a never-specified degree of liberty. There was the official notion, for example, that "media supervision," or *yulun jiandu*, as it is called in the official discourse, was necessary for the leadership to remain sufficiently informed. There was also the fact that controls on the media were largely exercised through post-facto discipline rather than prior censorship—meaning that editors could make calculated decisions about risk and run potentially sensitive stories. Communication researcher Maria Repnikova has referred to this dynamic as "guarded improvisation," in which "officials cautiously endorse media supervision as a feedback mechanism, as journalists carve out space for critical reporting by positioning themselves as aiding the agenda of the central state."[11]

For *Southern Weekly*, this "guarded improvisation" worked reasonably well, especially in the 1990s, when the local political climate in

Guangdong was relatively open and tolerant. According to former editor in chief Zuo Fang, senior leaders in Guangdong in the 1980s and 1990s, including Xie Fei and Lin Ruo, offered their support and protection for the newspaper. "Our hearts accord with those of Guangdong officials in charge of reform and opening up," Zuo Fang once said. He emphasized that this relatively harmonious relationship was based on four fundamental principles for the newspaper: (1) upholding the Communist Party's rule; (2) upholding current policies; (3) upholding the current political system; and (4) upholding social stability.

Therefore, *Southern Weekly*'s success, journalistically speaking, was never oppositional or necessarily antagonistic in nature. It resulted from bounded innovations that consciously carefully avoided opposition to the Communist Party. For a time, it seemed there was ample room to maneuver within the confines of media control. *Southern Weekly* and other commercialized outlets could expose corruption at the local level. They could question social injustices, insofar as they did not explicitly link them to questions about the legitimacy of the political system. They could encourage more active discussion on economic and cultural issues—though political issues always remained formally off-limits. And they could also provide valuable history and context, often from prominent academics, that served to elucidate current affairs.

One fact often overlooked in the lionizing of journalists at outlets like *Southern Weekly* as conscientious agitators for free speech, which we alluded to at the outset, is that their work requires interaction with the propaganda and control apparatus on a constant basis in order to negotiate the boundaries of critical reporting and commentary.

The breakthroughs of *Southern Weekly* in terms of content came with huge commercial success. Like print publications and online media elsewhere in the world, market-oriented outlets in China have relied on two major sources of revenue: subscription and advertising. Because *Southern Weekly* was among the first—and many would say, among the best—in providing attractive and relevant content, the newspaper attracted millions of readers across the country. Many of these readers were highly educated professionals in other emerging sectors of China's changing society, which meant a sizable and high-quality readership base that was attractive to advertisers. The most frequently seen advertisements appearing in *Southern Weekly* during its heyday in the 1990s and 2000s were from automobile companies. By the year 2000, at a time when China was still a largely undeveloped economy, *Southern Weekly*'s annual advertising revenue had already surpassed 100 million renminbi (RMB). The paper's most experienced journalists could earn salaries of around 10,000 RMB per month, at a time when the average annual salaries of urban residents in China were roughly the same amount.[12]

Competitive pay and a professional working environment meant that talent from across the country was drawn to *Southern Weekly*, in turn strengthening the position and reputation of the newspaper. The spirit of professionalism and social justice that *Southern Weekly* came to epitomize had complicated origins, but these included, as other scholars have noted, a long-standing liberal press tradition going back to at least the Republican Era and the late Qing dynasty, hand in hand with a deeper Confucian tradition that emphasizes the social and moral responsibility of the intellectual; and also Western theories of the role of the press, which have been used by Chinese journalists to resist the Maoist propaganda style.

WHAT HAPPENED IN 2012?

The real turning point for *Southern Weekly*, and for Chinese journalism more broadly, came in 2012. It was that year that two major incidents took place. First, because of the popularization of digital media and new social media platforms, the viable commercial model pursued by media in China for more than two decades, focused on circulation and advertising revenue, started to stagnate and decline. We'll deal further with this issue in the next section. Second, the Chinese Communist Party held its Eighteenth National Congress in November 2012, during which Xi Jinping became general secretary. While more freewheeling commercial media had by this point been a frequent thorn in the side of the leadership, epitomized by such cases as the Wenchuan Earthquake in May 2008 and the high-speed rail collision in Wenzhou in July 2011, Xi Jinping would soon make it clear that he intended to move far more aggressively than his predecessors to bring the media to heel, part of a much broader process of concentration and consolidation of power.

In the months leading up to the Eighteenth National Congress, *Southern Weekly* bore the brunt of the pressure applied to more conscientious media under a generally more hostile official environment for journalism. This pressure would culminate in the events described in this book—a rare outbreak of opposition that would become a defining moment for Xi in the first months of his leadership.

But first we should rewind to May 14, 2012, and the appointment of Tuo Zhen, the former vice president of China's official Xinhua News Agency, as provincial propaganda chief of Guangdong. Tuo's management style toward the media was significantly harsher than that of his predecessors in Guangdong, breaking the tacit consent that had long existed between censors and journalists and disturbing the delicate balance in government-press relations. The change quickly became evident to journalists at *Southern Weekly* and other local publications. The space for "guarded improvisation" shrank to an extent unprecedented in the newspaper's history.

In November 2012, on the eve of the Party's National Congress, carefully devised plans by *Southern Weekly* editors for related coverage were scuttled repeatedly by Tuo Zhen's propaganda department. The result was the production on the opening day of the National Congress of what many staffers regarded as one of the most disgraceful editions in the newspaper's history, which included a series of ten short and hastily prepared articles running over the first eight pages that sang the praises of the outgoing Hu Jintao administration. More crucially, Tuo had introduced new policies and procedures for content censorship, including the pre-review by propaganda officials of all major story topics before journalists could begin their work. This broke with the long-held tradition of post-facto discipline and enforced self-censorship—which for many years had allowed journalists a degree of discretion.

Another factor was the promotion, in December 2012, of Hu Chunhua to Guangdong's top leadership post of Party secretary. Though not directly involved in management of the media, Hu Chunhua exacerbated the worsening situation by neglecting to support Guangdong media as many of his predecessors had since the 1990s. Throughout his tenure in Guangdong, Hu would prove conservative and low-key, his priority being to avoid all missteps that might jeopardize his promotion within the central leadership.

By the end of 2012, the conditions were ripe for the boiling over of tensions at *Southern Weekly*; nearly all the factors that had led to the newspaper's rise had been eroded by political changes that were not yet in full evidence. By this time, nearly everyone in the newsroom felt a deep and abiding anger and resentment over the progressive loss of professional space. The final straw came with the production of *Southern Weekly*'s New Year's edition, due for release on January 1, 2013.

Among the fifty-two issues published each year by *Southern Weekly*, the year's first issue had long been the most valued and most anticipated, by both staff and readers. The New Year's commentaries, in particular, have been seen as standard-bearers of the paper's professional spirit and idealism, and many of these individual commentaries had left a deep impression even years later. The direct intrusion of Guangdong propaganda authorities into the editorial process of the New Year's edition of *Southern Weekly* in late December 2012 resulted not just in content that lacked the professional quality and gravity that was the paper's signature, but in content rife with rudimentary errors that many staffers found humiliating. The painful process of direct interference, and the loss of marginal autonomy it represented, were the catalysts that led most directly to the incident related in this book.

Guan Jun, the author of this story, formerly worked as a journalist at *Southern Weekly*. While he left the newspaper several years before the incident took place, he maintained close contact with the editors directly involved in the incident. He was, therefore, an outsider on the inside, and an insider on the outside—with a unique perspective on events. Guan is also an experienced writer and journalist in his own right. All of these factors make him, in our view, someone uniquely positioned to tell this version of the events surrounding the *Southern Weekly* incident.

WHERE IS CHINESE JOURNALISM NOW?

Ten years after the publication of the *Southern Weekly* editorial "Born in 1984," it is scarcely possible to imagine a media outfit with similar reach and influence in China daring a headline so loaded with political meaning. The reasons for this are of course partly political, driven by General Secretary Xi Jinping's uncompromising approach to media control and his broader consolidation of political power.

During a speech on February 19, 2016, following official visits to the Party's flagship *People's Daily* newspaper as well as China Central Television and Xinhua News Agency, Xi Jinping urged the imperative that media must be "surnamed Party," and must "love the Party, protect the Party and serve the Party." While Xi's speech focused on core media operated by the Party, it had broader implications for the media—and we should recall that publications like *Southern Weekly* are subsidiaries of the Party press system, and as such are subject to the same discipline. Xi said, referring to "guidance of public opinion," the notion that the Party must control the media in order to maintain social and political stability:

> In the various aspects and stages of news and public opinion work, [we must] adhere to the correct guidance of public opinion. Party newspapers and journals at various levels, and television and radio stations all must abide by correct guidance, and all metropolitan newspapers and magazines and new media must also abide by correct guidance. News reports must abide by correct guidance, and supplements, special programs, advertising and publicity must also abide by correct guidance; current affairs news must abide by correct guidance, and entertainment and social forms of the news must also abide by correct guidance; domestic news reports must abide by correct guidance, and international news reports must also abide by correct guidance. [13]

Xi Jinping's language makes an explicitly broad claim over all aspects of the media here, not just traditional print media, including metropolitan newspapers like *Southern Weekly*, and not just over breaking news, traditionally the priority focus of controls, but also over entertainment, advertising, and new media.

Xi Jinping's more robust approach to media controls has had a noticeable chilling effect on the practice of journalism in China. Commercial publications such as *Southern Weekly* were once at the heart of an always troubled but in many ways thriving movement of investigative reporting. But that movement, as such, is now a thing of the past, and investigative journalists can no longer find the strategic space they once had. [14] Hard news and on-the-ground reporting are also areas quite broadly impacted by the tightening environment for journalists. Breaking news stories, like the July 2011 Wenzhou rail collision, were points of insistent pressure by the professional media up to 2012, and in many instances media would explicitly ignore propaganda directives in order to report stories. This happens less frequently now, and prominent cases early in the Xi Jinping era, such as the Yangtze River cruise ship tragedy in June 2015, showed that the authorities could now dominate news coverage in ways that previously had been difficult.[15]

But the dawn of the Xi Jinping era at the end of 2012 also came at an inflection point for the business and technology of the media in China. Since the *Southern Weekly* incident, within the space of less than a decade, new digital platforms such as WeChat have come to dominate the media space, decisively upsetting the previous business models that nurtured commercial publications and paid for talent and top journalism. These new media technologies, while offering apparent choice to consumers, have also been a boon for the Chinese Communist Party, enabling more centralized control of information around broader notions like "cyber-sovereignty," and even turning news delivery devices, like smartphones, into tools of surveillance. This is a complex set of issues we won't address in detail here. But suffice it to say that the media ecology in China has transformed dramatically since Xi Jinping came to power, for political, commercial, and social reasons—and few of these changes, at least so far, have been a net positive for professional journalism.

Since the 2013 incident, *Southern Weekly* has experienced a free fall in terms of social influence, the amount of quality investigative reporting, and revenue. The general (and very sad) observation is that this newspaper is now a mediocre publication and is becoming increasingly irrelevant in the public life of the Chinese. Most of the journalists who were at *Southern Weekly* in 2013 have quit their jobs. Some of them remain in journalism and work for other more digitally focused outlets, but many more are now public relations specialists at rapidly growing internet companies such as Alibaba and ByteDance (the company that owns Jinri Toutiao and Douyin), helping to maintain the positive images of these tech giants. No longer are they focused on uncovering hidden truths and holding power accountable. None of the journalists featured in this book are still working at *Southern Weekly*.

Southern Weekly's fate is mirrored at other print publications across the country. We can say that the 2013 incident signaled in part the decline of print journalism in China, and since 2013 scores of newspapers and magazines have been shut down, including such reputable titles as the *Beijing Times*, the *Shanghai Evening Post*, the *Oriental*

Morning Post, the *International Herald Leader*, the *Outlook Magazine*, and the *Bund*. The advertising revenue of China's newspaper industry has declined at an annual rate of above 30 percent since 2014. For most traditional media outlets trying to make successful transitions, "media convergence" experiments have not for the most part been successful.

To put the China case in a broader context, we could say that the troubling times for *Southern Weekly* and other print media in China also reflect a global journalism crisis caused by technology innovations and the failure of existing business models. One crucial distinction, however, is that political controls on information in China, which are lately intensifying, have largely stymied any efforts to negotiate a new future for professional journalism using the tools and business models that the digital transition provides. The result of this hugely important shift is what one Chinese journalism professor recently termed, in a private conversation with the authors of this introduction, a "generational crisis in journalism," in which the professional gains Chinese media made over more than two decades are now rapidly being lost.

WHERE NOW?

If we take a slightly less pessimistic view of developments in China, we can note that journalism is still practiced in China, and that it is increasingly emerging at new digital platforms and through new types of content creators.

First, there are newly launched digital media projects sponsored by the Party-state, with the Shanghai-based *Pengpai* (or *The Paper*) being perhaps the most prominent example. A major caveat here, of course, is that *Pengpai* and its counterparts in other provinces have an explicit propaganda role to play, being deployed to "occupy the online public opinion field" by producing and disseminating content acceptable to the authorities that can at the same time go viral on the internet—especially among younger audiences. Their goal, then, is not to produce investigative journalism. At the same time, we should recognize that these media, like their precursors in the 1990s, are also driven to attract public interest and top talent, and this is often impossible without finding some room for critical reporting. As a result, *Pengpai* and similar digital publications produce a mix of sleek propaganda and serious journalism, including some influential investigative pieces that have triggered nationwide attention—and the subsequent intervention of censors. In 2015, *Pengpai* ran an in-depth investigative report on the environmental costs of the Three Gorges Dam that was many months in production but unfortunately was deleted soon after it was posted. In March 2016, the outlet broke a story about a national vaccine scandal exposing regulatory failures that enabled some doctors and drug dealers to illegally distribute more than $88 million in unrefrigerated and unsafe vaccines. After the story gained wide public attention, the propaganda department issued an order instructing other outlets not to rerun it.

Second, there is a new generation of media channels hosted by large internet portal websites such as Tencent, NetEase, and Sohu. Although they are not technically allowed to hire journalists to do original reporting, many of these channels still manage to push the envelope—"hitting line balls" is the Chinese phrase often used—and produce original content under the guise of the "special column," or through seemingly harmless genres such as "nonfiction writing." Some of the most prominent examples include Tencent's *Guyu* and NetEase's *Renjian*. In 2018, *Renjian* collaborated with independent journalist Huang Xueqin and exposed several sexual assault scandals amid China's #MeToo movement. Guyu also works with independent journalists, who in some cases have formed independent groups or collaboratives. One example is a team called Gushi Yinghe, an outfit for long-form journalism that includes many experienced journalists who used to work for traditional media outlets, including *Southern Weekly*.

Aside from these internet portals, there are a handful of tech websites in China that have also sought to produce serious journalism on social issues. One of the most prominent examples is Huxiu, which focuses on tech news but occasionally breaks out of this niche. In October 2018, Huxiu launched a special series called "New Women" that focused on gender equality in China.

Finally, there are hundreds of smaller and diverse players active on social media platforms that contribute to China's changing journalism landscape. They include individuals, volunteer groups, and small start-up companies. In August 2017, for example, a niche "publication" in the education industry called *Jiemodui* covered the mysterious death of a young man who had been involved in a pyramid scheme. In July 2018, a

WeChat public account called "Shouye" that focused on the real estate sector exposed yet another vaccine scandal. The founder of "Shouye," in fact, is a former *Southern Weekly* journalist. While the journalist no longer does investigative reporting on a regular basis, his efforts are part of a more dispersed and guerrilla-style approach to journalism we see emerging across a wider array of platforms.

Admittedly, all of these outlets and channels are working within a gray area, and it is always conceivable that their initiatives could be suppressed by the authorities. But Chinese journalism has always existed in the gray, and it does provide us with glimpses of various actors still working within the restrictions to advance their own professional and commercial agendas. As long as their work is tolerated, they continue to produce quality journalism that helps fill the void left by the decline of *Southern Weekly* and other media of the previous generation.

Finally, we should recognize and encourage the brave and professional reporting done in the midst of the novel coronavirus pandemic in 2020 by a small but decisive core of dedicated Chinese journalists. In-depth reports from such outlets as Caixin Media, Sanlian Life Weekly, Yicai Daily, the Economic Observer, Southern Metropolis Daily and China's People magazine, to name just a few, provided crucial details about the spread of the virus and about the failures and oversights in the official response. They offered more factual, authentic, and human perspectives on the epidemic and its impact, which often belied the official state narratives of unity, heroism, and faultless leadership. A few smaller start-up media initiatives focusing on public health such as Dingxiang Yisheng and Badian Jianwen provided science-based and policy-relevant reporting.

At some points in the crisis, there were even noticeable shades of the resistance seen during the Southern Weekly incident almost exactly seven years earlier—seen in the determined and creative resistance by Chinese media and internet users against both censorship and propaganda. One of the clearest examples came during Xi Jinping's March 10, 2020, visit to the city of Wuhan, the epicenter of the crisis, as positive state propaganda inundated the media space. Social media users in China struck back against the tide of falsehood by sharing an already censored cover story from People magazine in which Wuhan doctor Ai Fen shared her regrets at having allowed herself to be silenced by authorities in December 2019 over the true dangers of the emerging epidemic. As this damning story about the initial government cover-up was itself expunged from WeChat and other social media, users struck back by reposting it in myriad forms in attempts to elude censorship—using only emoticons, reading the entire story aloud on audio platforms, posting the story in romanized form, translating it into Korean (which could be auto-translated back into Chinese), and even rendering it in unique four-digit telegram codes.[16]

The title of this book is Silencing Chinese Media. In light of the complicated and ongoing contest between the taming force of the Party-state and the determination of professional journalists (and conscientious citizens) to expose the facts and make themselves heard, perhaps this title is best understood not as a pessimistic verdict, but rather as an open question about the future of Chinese voices—and their determination, against all odds, not to be silenced.

NOTES

1. Edward Wong, "Protest Grows over Censoring of China Paper," *New York Times*, January 7, 2013, https://www.nytimes.com/2013/01/08/world/asia/supporters-back-strike-at-newspaper-in-china.html.

2. Katie Hunt and CY Xu, "Chinese Journalists in Rare Protest against Censorship," CNN, January 7, 2013, https://edition.cnn.com/2013/01/07/world/asia/china-journalists-protests/index.html.

3. Adam Taylor, "A Chinese Censorship Scandal Is Spiraling Out of Control," *Business Insider*, January 9, 2013, https://www.businessinsider.com/southern-weekly-china-censorship-drama-2013-1.

4. "Sensitive Words: Southern Weekly Tempest," *China Digital Times*, January 7, 2013, https://chinadigitaltimes.net/2013/01/sensitive-words-southern-weekly-tempest-2.

5. US Department of State, Daily Press Briefing, January 7, 2013, https://2009-2017.state.gov/r/pa/prs/dpb/2013/01/202522.htm.

6. Minxin Pei, "China's Liberals Test Xi Jinping," *Wall Street Journal*, January 9, 2013, https://www.wsj.com/articles/SB10001424127887324081704578230931888941710.

7. David Bandurski, "Open Letter Ups the Ante on the Southern Weekly Incident," China Media Project, January 4, 2013, http://chinamediaproject.org/2013/01/04/open-letter-ups-the-ante-in-the-southern-weekly-incident.

8. Zhongdong Pan, "Bounded Innovations in the Media," in *Reclaiming Chinese Society: The New Social Activism*, ed. You-tien Hsing and Ching Kwan Lee (London: Routledge, 2009), 194.

9. Sharon LaFraniere and Jonathan Ansfield, "In Obama Interview, Signs of China's Heavy Hand," *New York Times*, November 19, 2009, https://www.nytimes.com/2009/11/20/world/asia/20china.html.

10. "China's News Reform to Promote Political Reform" (Zhongguo Xinwen Gaige Tuidong Zhengzhi Gaige), *Yazhou Zhoukan*, August 1, 2014, http://www.yzzk.com/cfm/content_archive.cfm?id=1368504021874&docissue=2004-31.

11. Maria Repnikova, *Media Politics in China: Improvising Power Under Authoritarianism* (Cambridge, UK: Cambridge University Press, 2017).

12. "Average Salary of Urban Workers Up 15.2 Percent in 2001," China.org.cn, June 11, 2002, http://german.china.org.cn/english/BAT/34316.htm.

13. "Xi Jinping's View of News and Public Opinion" (Xi Jinping de Xinwen Yulun Guan), *People's Daily Online*, February 25, 2016, http://politics.people.com.cn/n1/2016/0225/c1001-28147851.html.

14. Javier Hernandez, "'We're Almost Extinct': China's Investigative Journalists Are Silenced under Xi," *New York Times*, June 12, 2019, https://www.nytimes.com/2019/07/12/world/asia/china-journalists-crackdown.html.

15. David Bandurski, "Taming the Flood: How China's Leaders 'Guide' Public Opinion," *ChinaFile*, July 20, 2015, http://www.chinafile.com/reporting-opinion/media/taming-flood.

16. David Bandurski, "Whistling Against Deception," China Media Project, March 11, 2020, http://chinamediaproject.org/2020/03/11/whistling-against-deception.

PREFACE

The series of events known today as the "*Southern Weekly* affair" began as an internal dispute over editorial independence at one of China's most celebrated newspapers. In the end, it became the first and still the only moment since the pro-democracy protests of 1989 when public pressure challenged the Chinese Communist Party's media control system and openly pushed for greater freedom of expression. The brief but tumultuous days of this "affair" itself—as we at the paper experienced it—are the subject of this book. This is a factual account, and I hold myself personally responsible for the details reported here.

For me, the most compelling question lingering in the wake of these events is why things ended as they did. An answer to that question might help us explore other difficult questions. Why is our society like this? Is another kind of society not possible?

I benefited from so many acquaintances' assistance in putting this story together. Unfortunately, I must withhold many of their names for their safety. I would like to offer my heartfelt thanks to Dahui and Huiming, without whom this book would have been impossible.

✿ ✿ ✿

Note: The following text includes numerous chat records from WeChat. When necessary, I have disguised people's identities, using pseudonyms based on street names in Guangzhou.

MAIN CHARACTERS

There is a large cast of characters in this story. For readers' convenience, I have listed the most frequently mentioned characters in this book below, in the order in which they appear.

Ye Weimin, *Southern Weekly* editor
Cao Junwu, *Southern Weekly* editor
Yang Jibin, *Southern Weekly* editor
Shi Zhe, *Southern Weekly* editor
Su Yongtong, *Southern Weekly* editor
Tuo Zhen, Guangdong Province's propaganda minister
Huang Can, editor in chief, *Southern Weekly*
Wu Xiaofeng, deputy editor in chief, *Southern Weekly*
Yang Jian, Guangdong Province's deputy propaganda minister
Qin Xuan, *Southern Weekly* journalist
Chen Mingyang, deputy editor in chief, *Southern Weekly*
Jiang Yiping, veteran editor and senior Southern Media Group executive
Zeng Li, "special assistant" to the editors, *Southern Weekly*

1

BORN IN 1984

By mid-December the air in the southern city of Guangzhou had cooled at last to a lingering chill. Life slowed down and color faded from the city. The street-side restaurants, bustling into the early hours of the morning just a month earlier, grew quiet. Plants lost their blush amid a thickening haze that settled drearily over the city. The only touch of color that survived the winter came from the neon lights flashing from the business district's skyscrapers.

In the early morning hours of Thursday, December 20, 2012, a sea-blue Citroen sedan wound between these skyscrapers, heading south. Behind the wheel was Ye Weimin, an editor at *Southern Weekly*, a paper that for many embodied the spirit of reform that had transformed Guangzhou, and indeed the rest of China, over the previous thirty years. Together with Ye was the rest of *Southern Weekly*'s night shift editors: Cao Junwu, Yang Jibin, Shi Zhe, and Su Yongtong.

Their destination, Panyu, was Guangzhou's largest suburban district, located on the far south of the city, home to mile after mile of greenery broken only by high-rises and villas designed in an eclectic pseudo-European style.

Once these veteran editors had wrapped up an issue and signed off on the proofs, the mood inside the Citroen on the ride home to Panyu would usually be jovial. Conversation would often revolve around the online game Age of Empires, of which they were all aficionados. But that day, as Ye Weimin sped south over a river blanketed with fog, concern, frustration, and even anger weighed heavily on everyone's minds.

The shorthand term for their favorite pastime, *da diguo* (playing Empires), had taken on a new, distinctly bitter flavor. This was no longer just a game: *Southern Weekly* with its decades-old tradition of hard-hitting coverage—a fragile empire of idealism—was caught in a life-and-death struggle with Communist Party leaders who seemed hell-bent on destroying it.

Southern Weekly always had a reputation for pushing the envelope, covering sensitive news stories that tested the limits of tolerance under a Communist Party leadership anxious to maintain social and political control. The paper began as a spin-off of the Party-run *Nanfang Daily*, the official mouthpiece of the Guangdong leadership. Despite its formal connection to the government—a connection that all Chinese newspapers and magazines are required to have—*Southern Weekly* had defined its own mission. The founders of *Southern Weekly*, liberal thinkers within the Party, wanted to break with a media system in which a handful of officially controlled papers dominated all news and commentary.

Launched in 1984, in the early years of China's economic reform era, the newspaper's motto was "There may be truths that we cannot tell, but we steadfastly refuse to tell lies." This was indeed still a compromise, but nevertheless a brave and significant compromise. Working within the limits of an authoritarian political system, *Southern Weekly* strove to be a voice for enlightenment and new ideas.

Despite its roots in the Party-state media monopoly, *Southern Weekly* was also part of an initial reorientation of Chinese media toward the market that would eventually accelerate further in the 1990s. *Southern Weekly* was not subsidized by the state but survived commercially by exploring the frontiers of an emerging media marketplace—if readers bought the paper, the paper could sell space to advertisers. *Southern Weekly* did not need subsidies from the state, and in fact brought in revenue for its Party-run "mother paper," *Nanfang Daily*. At its pinnacle, *Southern Weekly*'s circulation exceeded one million.

This model had been replicated across China by the end of the 1990s. Commercial newspapers became cash cows for tired Party mouthpieces. Many of these spin-offs grew restless with the passage of time, testing the waters with ever bolder news coverage, driven forward

by both their professional ideals and the market's rewards for real journalism. Nowhere was this restiveness more evident than at *Southern
Weekly*, which over the years became a bastion of journalistic professionalism and forward-thinking idealism—anathema within a political
system that saw the media serving not the public, but only the Party.

Southern Weekly's independent streak had repeatedly made it a target of criticism and discipline from propaganda officials over the years.
In wave after wave of purges, editors and reporters had come and
gone—many of them moving on to become senior figures at other major media, carrying on the "*Southern Weekly* spirit." But the paper had
managed to weather all these storms, even in 2003 when the authorities
tried to bring it to heel by installing a provincial propaganda official,
Zhang Dongming, in a senior managerial role. Despite such interven-
tions, *Southern Weekly* was still widely respected, even beyond China's
borders. When US president Barack Obama made a state visit to China
in 2009, his aides refused an interview with the state television network,
China Central Television, opting instead for an interview with *Southern
Weekly*.

Purges had long been standard fare at *Southern Weekly*. Further
penalties had always hung, like the Sword of Damocles, over the head
of the paper, for this or that perceived violation of "propaganda discipline." But that night as the editors drove south, the situation was worse
than it had ever been. It was as if a permanent winter had set in since
the previous spring. And that winter had a name: Tuo Zhen.

Tuo Zhen had arrived in Guangzhou from Beijing in May 2012,
appointed a member of Guangdong Province's Party Standing Committee and its Chief Minister of Propaganda. Immediately upon arriving,
Tuo Zhen made it his mission to rein in Guangzhou's outspoken press,
with a particular focus on *Southern Weekly*. In the past, censorship had
typically operated from outside the paper, with the propaganda department sending down regular guidelines on taboo topics to avoid. This
approach placed certain issues and stories off-limits, but also left open a
vast, unexplored territory where media could pursue stories strategically. Yet in recent years, a much more aggressive system of internal prepublication and even pre-writing review and censorship of story topics
had emerged. And under Tuo Zhen's leadership this trend was growing
ever more intrusive. Articles were gutted by appointed in-house censors
or removed wholesale at the proofing stage. Propaganda officials vetted

proposed story topics, nipping potential problems in the bud. Every shrinking inch of space to cover real news was now disappearing.

On the road to Panyu that night, the editors talked strategy, a kind of offline "playing Empires" for the real world. What could be done about Tuo Zhen? They might, one suggested, write a sternly worded open letter with another newspaper in the province facing editorial pressures, announcing the intention of staff from both publications to resign unless Tuo stepped down.

Another possibility was for *Southern Weekly* to publish an investigative story on something so horrific that it was sure to cause a public stir—for example, a report on organ harvesting from China's death-row inmates. Once provincial propaganda authorities inevitably killed the report, they could post it online and ride a wave of public anger against their censors and Tuo Zhen.

Schemes and stratagems were batted back and forth inside the tiny car until finally everyone fell silent. The possibilities dangled playfully before them, like ornaments on a rearview mirror. But everyone looked ahead with a sense of foreboding.

2

WINTER COMES SOUTH

Coming home from the late shift, Cao Junwu typically fell asleep right away. He was always burned out by this point in the week. And if it weren't for the call to play Age of Empires with colleagues the next evening, he would have preferred to remain asleep—to be honest, even nightmares were preferable to a typical day at work.

All five editors were unrepentant homebodies. Other than the two or three days they had to spend at the newspaper every week, none cared to set foot in the city, with its hustle and bustle. Shi Zhe grew organic vegetables on his patio and Su Yongtong, the bachelor, had a full garden. Panyu provided them with an escape from the pressures that haunted them at work.

Cao Junwu was a good-looking guy. His short hair was always a bit unkempt, and he was built like a flagpole, tall and skinny. But what really stood out most about him was his perpetual laziness. It was typically 4:00 or 5:00 in the afternoon before he crawled out of bed, and he would always preface his chats on the WeChat instant messaging service with the warning "Still waking up." His username on Sina Weibo was "Lazybug Cao."

The other editors weren't quite as lazy, but neither could you say they were full of spunk. Despite their generally slacker approach to life, they were dedicated to their work at *Southern Weekly* even at the most trying of times.

In Cao Junwu's view, the general dejectedness they all felt was a product of the environment in which they worked and its tensions with their ideals. Most of the editorial staff had been born in the era of reforms (after 1980) and were in their early to mid-twenties at that point. They came of age in a China opening to the world, developing rapidly, and approaching normality. However, they had just missed the "golden decade" of relative openness in the 1980s, when there was unprecedented exploration in media and culture in general. Instead, the early years of their youth coincided with the "lost decade" of the 1990s, in which cultural policy was considerably tightened in the aftermath of the state violence of 1989. If there was anything that invited their hatred or contempt, it was the lies they had been forced to read in the state media from an early age. As a result, *Southern Weekly* was far more than just a paycheck for them.

For Shi Zhe, Su Yongtong, and Cao Junwu, working at *Southern Weekly* was their dream. The paper had been their first choice for a career, as was also true for Xiao Hua, Zhu Hongjun, and other members of the paper's editorial team.

Cao Junwu remembered colleagues often saying, "We can't just let this paper's legacy die in our hands." Before Tuo Zhen had arrived in Guangzhou, such a statement had been more about a sense of responsibility to *Southern Weekly*'s values. But now, with Tuo Zhen's dark shadow hanging over the paper, keeping this legacy alive took on much greater urgency.

In retrospect, Tuo Zhen's shadow could be seen in many *Southern Weekly* moments from 2012.

That July, when huge storms flooded Beijing and caused at least seventy-nine deaths, *Southern Weekly* dispatched reporters to cover the story. The result was eight full pages of reports focusing on the victims and subtly pointing to the glaring deficiencies in city planning and management that had led to these deaths. During the internal review process, provincial propaganda authorities made their demands clear: the reports must praise public servants who had died in the line of duty; other victims of the floods were not to be mentioned. The editors were left feeling that the only way they could maintain their journalistic integrity was to avoid reporting this event at all, even if doing so was also a great disservice to their readers.

There had been other moments in 2012 when avoiding a topic was simply not possible. When the Chinese Communist Party held its Eighteenth Party Congress that November, with Hu Jintao handing over power to Xi Jinping, the transition became an opportunity for Tuo Zhen and provincial propaganda officials to prove just how effectively they had tamed the once freewheeling *Southern Weekly*. A directive from the authorities ordered the newspaper to devote most of its coverage to the Eighteenth Party Congress, with the added requirement that coverage must praise social "harmony" and the wisdom of the Party. The issue that resulted from these orders, filled with effusive praise for the Party, was viciously mocked by internet users as "even more *People's Daily* than *People's Daily*." The five members of the editorial team had recused themselves from the final stages of editing that issue in a mini-strike. This gesture, however, could not stop the "reddest" edition of *Southern Weekly* in its three-decade history from hitting the newsstands.

After the Eighteenth Party Congress, new Chairman Xi Jinping made his first provincial visit to Guangdong. This move seemed to echo the footsteps of reform pioneer Deng Xiaoping, whose "southern tour" in 1992 had broken through rigid post-1989 resistance to further economic reforms. Was Xi's visit a signal that further opening was on the way? Staff at *Southern Weekly* would eventually look back on their eager expectations at this moment and chuckle at their naïve optimism. They had excitedly prepared two huge reports on Xi Jinping's "southern tour," with the possibility that they could be violating the Party's core narrative never once crossing their minds. The provincial propaganda office, however, vetoed the reports outright, leaving no room for discussion. In the end, the front page of the paper featured only a large picture of Xi's visit, with a headline and a few sweeping generalizations, coming to just 299 characters. This was the newspaper's shortest front-page report in memory—if it could even be called a report.

In 2012, *Southern Weekly* had a total of 1,034 news reports or articles canceled or subjected to major changes, an average of twenty articles per edition. Without a doubt, the cold winds that now left everyone at the paper shivering in anxiety had arrived that spring with Tuo Zhen.

"There were some pretty major events that year. I would always have Tang Min, an editorial staffer, take my drafts to the internal examiner. I would feel so uneasy, not knowing at all what changes I could expect to come back. Sometimes the proofs were awash with red, as though my reports had undergone some type of violent assault," said Su Yongtong, the editor of the paper's legal news section. Hailing from Fujian, struggling to speak Mandarin, Su would always go to great lengths to explain what he meant clearly. As he reflected on his lengthy back-and-forth sessions with the censors, his emotions would start to show. "Toward the end, I would be so exhausted that I became cowardly and complacent. I really worried that I could grow accustomed to this kind of environment and become ever number—that all I could ever do was back down."

Southern Weekly's signature was the in-depth investigative report; reporters and editors would go to any length to get every detail just right. But after all that effort, a report could be killed without explanation. "Imagine a snail crossing the road, dragging himself along for half a day," recalled reporter Zhou Hualei. "He's almost there, almost to the end, and then—BAM—suddenly someone comes along and steps on him." That's what it was like preparing a report under Tuo Zhen.

This sudden "winter in the south," as some called it, wasn't all that difficult to comprehend. China had been in a process of transition from Maoist totalitarianism for nearly three decades. However, because political reforms had stalled while economic reforms proceeded, economic and political power became intertwined. Within the halls of power, powerful and very conservative interest groups, dedicated solely to protecting their own power and interests at whatever cost, had emerged. Any media reports that did not cast this autocratic system in the most positive light came to be viewed as "sensitive." This sensitivity caused nervousness; nervousness spawned hostility; hostility spawned rage. And when it came time for officials to act on this rage, they often targeted *Southern Weekly*.

Staff at *Southern Weekly* also found their own ways of venting their anger at the constant indignities they suffered at the hands of propaganda officials. Some vented their feelings on the paper's internal messaging boards or on Sina Weibo. Meetings were even held with superiors. But the justifications were always the same, whether they came from the editor in chief, Huang Can, or provincial propaganda officials. A political meeting as important as the Eighteenth Party Congress could not be handled casually. Once the congress was over, they promised, things would naturally loosen up a bit. As always, however, the better, more open tomorrow promised by officials never materialized.

As the end of the year approached, the most important task on everyone's radar was the New Year's edition, an always eagerly awaited issue. As planning for this issue proceeded that year, a few staffers began to have ominous feelings. Yang Jibin wrote the following in a post in *Southern Weekly*'s "Ark Forum" chat group on December 28, 2012:

> Summing up what we've seen over the past year, I think my colleagues and I have committed the error of thinking those up top want to censor us, when in fact they want to kill us off.
>
> If it were just a matter of censorship, it's a matter of back-and-forth, of testing the waters, of gaming the other side, of pressure and compromise. It's like a game, all too familiar to us. But lately, this familiar game has been replaced with verbal abuse, orders, and a demand for obedience. The intrusions on our work seem to worsen by the day. Yes, the goal, it seems, is to kill *Southern Weekly*.
>
> They had said before that things would loosen up after the Eighteenth Party Congress. But the Congress has come and gone, and we are still required to report our story topics to provincial propaganda officials every week. Topics for the New Year's special edition have already been completely gutted. And now, of those topics fortunate enough to survive this initial carnage, who could say how many would ultimately make it to the newsstand?
>
> There are two things that help a paper to stand out from the competition: exclusive reports and special issues. We no longer have any chance of publishing exclusives in this environment, and now our New Year's special edition is coming under the knife. The Provincial Propaganda Department's approach can no longer be simply classified as "censorship." Their actions and their attitude already made clear that they have only one thing in mind: killing us off completely.
>
> In any case, the New Year's edition is the main business at hand at the moment. It is the final task for editors to complete for 2012— and the first task for 2013.
>
> In the current environment, I have no hope of pushing for any type of change. I can only hope to keep this paper alive, to pass it on to others who may be stronger than we are today.
>
> If they manage to turn our New Year's edition into total garbage, then we will go down along with it. We'll do whatever it takes.

3

KILLS, CUTS, EDITS, REMOVALS

Writing now, it would be a useless exercise to try to make readers guess what changes might occur in China in 2013. This was, however, the theme of our "Ten Big Guesses for 2013" feature at the beginning of that year. Since 2013 is now long past, let's try a different game instead—can readers guess which of our guesses for 2013 were eliminated by the provincial propaganda authorities as unfit for the general public? The answer may surprise you.

"Ten Big Guesses for the New Year" had been a special part of our New Year's edition for the past five years. We would take big, lofty ideals and wrap them up in fun and relatable packaging. It was always a hit with the readers. While preparing "Ten Big Guesses for 2013," the editor in charge, Shi Zhe, decided it would be safest to prepare eleven, just in case propaganda officials saw a problem with one of the related pieces. Our topics were:

1. Will there be new progress toward realizing rule of law?
2. Will there be a relaxation of the reeducation through labor (*laogai*) system?
3. Will the there be a relaxation of the One-Child Policy, implementing a two-child policy nationally?
4. Will other provinces begin pilot projects on the public reporting of officials' assets?
5. Will there be reforms to the income distribution system?
6. Will peace be maintained in China's seas?

7. Will there be an end to local preferential policies in the college entrance examination?
8. Can China's stock market pass the 3,000 mark?
9. Will property prices rebound?
10. Will a Nobel Prize in the sciences be awarded to a Chinese citizen?
11. Will more countries begin accepting Chinese tourists visa-free?

On December 24, the plan for the New Year's edition was sent to the provincial propaganda office. Two days later, the editors received their response: Will there be a relaxation of the One-Child Policy? There cannot be any speculation about this. Will there be a relaxation of the labor reeducation system? There cannot be any speculation about this. Will other provinces begin pilot programs in the reporting of officials' assets? There cannot be any speculation about this. Will there be an increase in the number of visa-free countries for Chinese tourists? There cannot be any speculation about this.

In one fell swoop, four of Shi Zhe's topics had been killed. Shocked, he pulled together one more topic firmly in the safe zone—which made for the eight topics that were eventually published. Shi Zhe decided to keep the headline "Ten Guesses for the New Year" with a disclaimer: "Due to limited operating capacity, we could only come up with eight."

Work on the New Year's special edition finally came to an end just one hour before the year ended. On the twenty-third floor of their office building, the editors sat back smoking, the burning tips of their cigarettes flickering like the paper's trademark neon sign outside. The last step before the issue was sent to the printer was approval from propaganda officials. Everyone wondered just what would be cut next.

The cuts and kills had come one after the other over the previous week and showed no signs of abating. The first round arrived on December 26, in the planning stage. Aside from the four "guess" topics mentioned above, three people profiled in a section called "Turning Dreams into Reality" were rejected. The first was Ren Jianyu, a graduate of Chongqing University who became a village official after graduation. Ren had been sent to a labor reeducation facility for a satirical poem he had posted online. Then there was a rational patriot who showed his love for China in a "reasonable" (i.e., nondestructive) way during anti-Japanese marches in Guangzhou. Finally, there was well-known Peking University scholar Qian Liqun, a proponent of humanism. Propaganda officials also voiced their reservations about a fourth possibility, Zhang Xiaolong, known as WeChat Zhang, responsible for new product development at the tech giant Tencent.

"Showing one's love for one's country in a rational way. Could there be anything with greater 'positive energy' (*zheng nengliang*) than that?" one of the editors asked, jokingly employing Xi Jinping's latest buzzword, "positive energy."

The heart of the special edition—the annual New Year's greeting— had not been killed all at once. Its journey was long and tortuous, beset with trouble. Several years earlier, *Southern Weekly* had begun profiling important contributors to contemporary society as "Torchbearers of the Chinese Dream." Soon after coming to power, Xi Jinping had also begun to talk about the idea of a "Chinese Dream," a term which was then immediately celebrated throughout state media. Accordingly, everyone at *Southern Weekly* agreed that nothing could be safer than making the "Chinese dream" the theme of the New Year's issue. Unfortunately, it turned out that provincial propaganda officials felt that now that Xi Jinping had adopted the idea, *Southern Weekly* no longer had any right to comment on the "Chinese Dream."

At first, writers had wanted to use the idea of the "Chinese Dream" to talk about "a dream of freedom" in the New Year's greeting. Propaganda officials unsurprisingly rejected this. Next, the writers wanted to interpret the "Chinese Dream" as the "dream of constitutionalism." This, again, was rejected. After a round of back-and-forth, the best the writers hoped for was to allude to how difficult it was to realize the Chinese Dream. Again, this was rejected. Finally, the headline was changed to reflect an entirely different meaning: "We are now closer than ever to realizing the Chinese Dream." According to Dai Zhiyong, who penned the first draft, 90 percent of this draft—already written under the topical restrictions of propaganda officials—was eventually deleted or rewritten beyond recognition. The content added to the greeting celebrated the happy lives of the people and praised the Party.

The travails over this issue had been longer and more trying than anything the editors had previously suffered under Tuo Zhen's already torturous watch. As the year literally drew to an end and they awaited final approval, the five editors felt the knife being twisted. They were exhausted. The editor in chief, Huang Can, had been seen taking pictures of the final proofs with his mobile phone. Who knows who he had sent them to?

Just after midnight, literally just minutes into the New Year, the editors received notification from Huang Can that a new set of directives had come from propaganda officials. Two of the directives were particularly puzzling. The first was the demand to replace the image they had chosen for the front page of the newspaper, a classical image of Yu the Great taming the floods, with an image of China's new aircraft carrier. The second demand was to remove the already heavily re-edited piece about Guangzhou's "rational patriot." Soon a fierce argument broke out. The editors surrounded Huang Can, interrogating him about the absurd rationale behind these decisions—supposedly, the black-and-white traditional ink painting was too gray in tone, and the clothes worn by people in the painting were too ragtag. Cao Junwu shouted excitedly, "With this kind of mindset, anything could be a problem!" The angry back-and-forth went on for nearly an hour, until Huang Can finally accepted the editors' determination to keep the image.

Then, suddenly, the next directive came. Another report had to be removed: a profile of Zhang Jing, the wife of a street vendor named Xia Junfeng who faced the death penalty for killing two urban patrol officers (*chengguan*) in what many saw as an act of self-defense. The special edition looked increasingly like a barren tree that was now losing its branches, one by one. The editors had originally planned a sixteen-page issue, but it had now been cut down to twelve.

The back-and-forth over seemingly every detail of the issue continued until about 3:00 a.m., when Huang Can finally said, "Ok, we'll leave it like this for the moment." Generally, the editing process for the New Year's special edition required that all five editors sign off on each of the twelve pages of the proofs. After that, deputy editor in chief Wu Xiaofeng would sign off, marking the end of the process. Everyone signed wearily, as if they knew this was only a tentative peace agreement with an ever-more-confident aggressor.

The temperature that night gradually crept toward zero, and the moon hung cold over Guangzhou's skyscrapers. At the Shaxian Delicacies snack shop next to the *Southern Weekly* offices, the five editors sat frozen in shock, huddled over their warm dishes. None had any hope for the New Year that had just arrived.

It was not hard for them to see that the troubles facing this edition were hardly over, but the five main editors had already made their decision—now that they had signed off on what should be the final version of this issue, they would have nothing more to do with it. Wu Xiaofeng had told them: "After you sign, go straight home. Turn off your phones. Get some sleep."

There was no hope, however, of Wu Xiaofeng turning off his phone and getting some sleep. Just a few hours later, he and Huang Can were called to the offices of the Provincial Propaganda Department to hear the latest orders.

Provincial propaganda authorities have their own building in Guangzhou. There is no sign on the door identifying their offices. They are housed in one of those old, symmetrical, completely nondescript buildings, showing no hint of design, but surrounded by shrubs and flowers that filled the place with a sleepy aroma.

Huang Can and Wu Xiaofeng learned, not entirely to their surprise, that the New Year's edition still did not have final approval. Among the "new" directives was a demand, yet again, that the front-page image be replaced with an aircraft carrier.

In the eyes of most editors and reporters at *Southern Weekly*, Huang Can was a servant of the Party propaganda system, the faithful executor of its will. Wu Xiaofeng too was someone who seldom spoke out in defense of the paper's ideals. But this time, even Huang and Wu could not stand to accept the propaganda officials' demands. After some discussion, a compromise was finally reached: the size of the front-page image would be reduced, and a paragraph of text would be added to mitigate against any "misinterpretation" of the intended message.

Yu the Great Taming the Floods is a traditional-style Chinese painting rich in detail and dark in tone, commissioned by the editors specifically for the cover of the New Year's edition at a price of 1,500 RMB. Every detail in the painting has the feel of a rough, jagged edge. Yu the Great was the mythical leader of an alliance of clans four thousand years ago, and he is regarded in China as a hero who earned the title of emperor not through the usual path of inheritance but rather as a meritocratic reward for his courage and quick thinking. He was remembered and praised by those who came after primarily for his new ideas about dealing with seasonal floods—he advocated dredging and removing obstructions to the waters rather than building up further dams and obstructions.

In history, the metaphor of water has often been used to refer to the common people. Their anger, in turn, is described as a flood. There is a long-standing tradition in Chinese culture of making one's point in an esoteric manner, a special kind of skill and wit in artistic representation fostered under authoritarian rule. The editors at *Southern Weekly* were thus fond of this painting of Yu the Great not just because it was a breathtaking image. China was now entering a period of great social tension, and anger—a flood—was building. Facing this flood, the editors felt that the authorities should learn from Yu the Great, finding ways to accommodate divergent views and criticisms rather than simply building barriers. Propaganda officials were also attuned to the implications of the cover photo, and ironically, not learning from Yu, wanted to build barriers to hide this message away.

It did not matter at all to propaganda officials that the editors felt that this issue's New Year's greeting had already been effectively destroyed. For *Southern Weekly*, China's most celebrated weekly newspaper, the New Year's special edition was a tradition going back more than a decade. The New Year's greeting on this issue's front page had grown into something of a cultural institution, with some of the most memorable titles of years past engraved in the minds of the public. Some examples of classics that stood the test of time include the exhortation to "Let the powerless find strength, and the pessimists march ahead" and "There are those powers that send tears streaming down our faces," both published in 1999; or "A single word of truth is of greater gravity than the entire world," published in 2006. Such words of inspiration and exhortation, first published in *Southern Weekly*'s New Year's issue, had become popular catchphrases. But propaganda officials saw nothing but danger in such words.

Yang Jian suggested that Yu the Great taming the flood needed to be brought "in line with the Party spirit, and in line with the spirit of economic reforms." Wu Xiaofeng made note of this and drafted a blurb of about one hundred words on his mobile phone, which he immediately messaged to Zheng Guangning. "In this process, it was never clear who would be making decisions, or at which level of the bureaucracy," Wu Xiaofeng later recalled.

On the night of January 1, the revised content of the New Year's greeting that had already been signed off on was ordered to be re-sent to a designated inbox. That night, Zheng Guangning sent Wu Xiaofeng the altered introduction via text message. Aside from this, the Provincial Propaganda Department telephoned with a directive: the main heading of the special issue, "Homeland Dreams," was to be changed to "Pursuing Dreams." A few more sentences were to be cut from the New Year's greeting, and other content was to be added at their request—once again, they were cutting here and rewriting there.

It was impossible to refuse these endless changes. On January 2, Huang Can and Wu Xiaofeng tried to reach the five editors responsible for the special issue. Shi Zhe recalls that the phone call from Wu Xiaofeng seemed more like a courtesy call, just to let him know. Shi felt that if the changes went against the original intention of the editors, then it shouldn't bear their names at all any longer. Waking up on the afternoon of January 2, Cao Junwu also saw an incoming call from Wu Xiaofeng, but he let it go unanswered. Hearing about all that happened from Shi Zhe, Cao sent a text message to Wu asking that he please defend the editors' bottom line.

With the editors responsible for the issue refusing to participate in any further changes, Huang Can and Wu Xiaofeng made changes on their own. This included removing the entire article on the young Guangzhou patriot that writers had once imagined as a sign of "positive energy." They were just doing as instructed. As there was now a three-page hole in the issue, this empty space was filled in with ads for the newspaper group. The New Year's issue, altered beyond recognition, did not in the end bear the names of the paper's editors.

4

FLOODWATERS RISING

In the old mountainous town of Lijiang in China's southwest Yunnan province, there is a small guesthouse hidden away in a back alley. The owner is Yu Chen, the former chief editor of the investigative news department at *Southern Weekly*. Yu Chen had been forced to part ways with the newspaper in late May 2012, after a report infuriated propaganda officials. In January 2013 he was living a quiet life in Yunnan, where the corpus of exposés he had planned and executed during his time at *Southern Weekly* was a distant yet painful memory. He wasn't sure whether to blame Tuo Zhen for ending his career in journalism, or thank him.

During the New Year's holiday, Yu's guesthouse was an unusually busy place. Members of *Southern Weekly*'s in-depth news department, both past and present, had come for an end-of-year celebration. It was a time to relax and recuperate—but there was also a strong sense of camaraderie, like seasoned veterans of war gathering again in peacetime.

Qin Xuan, who worked in *Southern Weekly*'s international news department, had joined the retreat. On the evening of January 2, Qin, fiddling on his mobile, noticed several images posted to "Image Work," an invitation-only WeChat group set up by members of the *Southern Weekly* team. The group was named "Image Work" to poke fun at the actions of propaganda officials ahead of the Eighteenth Party Congress in November 2012: many reports had been killed, and the resulting empty spaces in the paper were filled with innocuous images. But today in this group, Qin saw a few not-so-innocuous images: the latest proofs of the endlessly altered New Year's edition.

"I was totally furious," Qin later recalled with his straight-talking Beijing style.

On the way to dinner that evening, Qin Xuan discussed the endless alterations with his fellow journalists. He suggested that colleagues who no longer worked at the paper post news about the changes on Sina Weibo. In his words, "It wouldn't be ideal for someone still at *Southern Weekly* to post this."

The group crowded into a dimly lit halal restaurant, pulled up their chairs, and settled elbow to elbow around two small tables. Everyone there, whose lives at one time or another had been linked intimately with *Southern Weekly*, felt angry about the propaganda officials' blatant interference in the paper's operations. Wang Xing and Xiao Dang were the first to post the news on Weibo. According to Xiao Dang's recollection, he was just a few seconds ahead of Wang Xing, but Wang's post was "a bit more detailed" and was shared far more widely.

Qin Xuan hardly touched his meal that night. He was busy monitoring events as they unfolded on Weibo. "Even if it meant resigning and leaving the paper," he said, "I knew we had to see this through to the end."

Looking back on that night and the events that followed, no one involved could have imagined that a few Weibo posts complaining about propaganda officials' interference could suddenly become such a rallying point.

The magnitude of the eventual response to these events actually wasn't due to outrage at adversity and injustice. Rather, it was triggered by the tragicomic absurdity of the very different narratives of the events shared on Weibo, a real-time, interactive multimedia tool that played a central role in these events. Once a valuable piece of information was posted there, it would spread like a hyper-contagious virus. And just as an infectious disease mutates while it spreads, so information transmitted via Weibo was also prone to its own mutations.

Online, the earliest description of the events at *Southern Weekly* went something like this: A deputy provincial-level official had taken advantage of the holiday to deceive the editors, radically altering the annual greeting in *Southern Weekly*'s New Year's special edition and even adding an entire paragraph of text on the front page. In the process of transmission, embellished versions appeared, saying for example that the official had "sneaked into the proof room," even according to some accounts "in his pajamas."

Another unexpected detail gave the story wings in the online world—the very rare surname of Guangdong's propaganda minister: Tuo. The name "Tuo" lit up the chatter over ongoing developments at *Southern Weekly*, inviting endless wordplay thanks to the homophonic nature of the Chinese language. The surname "Tuo," for example, was substituted with another character for *tuo*, an adjective with scatological overtones. Others used another version of *tuo*, meaning "ostrich," calling up images of a gangly and awkward bird that hides its head in the sand. The possibilities were endless, resulting in a kind of online free-for-all.

On their official Weibo accounts, various Chinese media outlets responded to these revelations by trying to outdo one another with their satirical references to Tuo Zhen. Incredibly, even official media like Xinhua News joined in the exercise—all the more unfathomable considering that Tuo Zhen had been deputy director of Xinhua before he was "sent down south" as Guangdong's new propaganda minister.

> @XinhuaViewpoint [Xinhua Weibo Commentary]. When it meets with danger, the ostrich buries its head in the sand, believing itself to be safe this way. "Problems," they say, "are the voice of an age." In fact, the deliberate avoidance of problems is a huge issue we face in the era of reform. Using one's public authority to intimidate and suppress private interests, making problems worse—that is even more extreme than the ostrich who only buries its head in the sand. Reform means we must lift our heads and face problems head on. Reform is about resolving problems. Reporter Liu Yang.

The unforeseen response on social media had an unexpected chemical reaction with the pent-up emotions inside *Southern Weekly*. Cao Junwu recalled, "We had endured the situation for half a year, and anger ran deep. The New Year's edition became a turning point, and the whole saga wore us all out. The crux of the matter was that the New Year's special edition was one of the paper's treasured legacies, a tradition passed down from one generation to the next. Could we allow that to be ruined?"

Just a few hours after the first eruption on social media, a second explosion burst through cyberspace, provoking even more widespread interest. Once readable images of the edition were posted online, people discovered multiple glaring errors in the text. The edition number had been printed incorrectly. In the introductory text, last-minute additions by propaganda officials had produced glaring errors—the phrase "unity of will is an impregnable stronghold" had been rendered with the wrong final character, a homophone with a different and indeed completely incoherent meaning. And the fabled episode of Yu the Great taming the waters was written as having happened two thousand years ago instead of four thousand years. This was a grade-school error akin to *Time* magazine asserting that Eisenhower had commanded the Invasion of Normandy during the American Civil War.

These laughable errors combined with tales of propaganda officials interfering with the editorial process to turn the *Southern Weekly* story into a captivating drama. Discussions of monstrous, arrogant, and ignorant high-level Party propaganda officials spread like wildfire online.

The Nanfang Press Group complex at 289 Guangzhou Avenue, home of *Southern Weekly*, *Southern Metropolis Daily*, and other leading commercial media, was the premiere training ground for journalists involved in market-oriented media in China. Many who had started there had gone on to become the backbone of other well-regarded newspapers and magazines. These *Southern Weekly* veterans felt a uniquely strong sense of responsibility toward the paper and all that it represented. The top news editor of one major web portal told his former colleagues at *Southern Weekly*: "We've been ordered not to report on this, but we're resisting this order."

Media organizations that had similar experiences of torment by propaganda officials wanted to show their support but also needed to do so in the safest way possible. Several major internet news portals, for example, ran classic *Southern Weekly* reports and commentaries.

In these early hours of what would become known as the "*Southern Weekly* affair," the internet was brimming with inventive responses. There was even an online movement challenging netizens to compose their own versions of the paper's annual New Year's greeting. Such activities openly mocked propaganda officials while showing solidarity with embattled editors.

In the Web 2.0 era, and particularly in the era of Weibo, anyone could break news. Everyone had been woven together in a giant media network. This also meant that hundreds of millions of users could experience firsthand the obsessive information control regime: "this Weibo post has already been deleted." All at once during this New Year's holiday, students, professionals, academics, and all other types of Chinese citizens, angered by the violation of their right to know and the limitation of their freedom of expression, could no longer hold back.

There is an old saying derived from an ancient classic of Chinese political philosophy, *The Discourses of the States*: "It is more dangerous to stop the free flow of people's thoughts than to stop the flow of a river." This saying also resonates with the myth of Yu the Great taming the floods. Both speak to the long-standing sense of dread rulers in China feel about the risks of anger and outrage that are destined to build up within an authoritarian system, as well as the uncontrollable nature of this anger once it reaches a breaking point.

In the online world, floods are silent. They do not destroy homes or uproot trees. But their speed and scale are even greater than in the real world. The flood pictured on the front page of the New Year's edition of *Southern Weekly* had not happened two thousand or four thousand years ago—it was happening in the present.

Tuo Zhen was one essential rock in the Communist Party's vast dam attempting to stop this flood from surging forth. During the *Southern Weekly* affair, public opinion burst forth, momentarily overwhelming him.

"I didn't feel there was anything particularly noteworthy about these changes, and it never occurred to me that everyone would come together in a movement like this," reporter Fang Kecheng later recalled. "It's really exciting to have experienced. My specialty is in reporting the news, but in this case, I found us at the center of the news."

Staffers were eager for vengeance: most wanted to use the situation to force a way out of the crisis looming over the paper in recent months. They wanted to press Huang Can to step down, and to cast off Tuo Zhen's strict controls.

It was after 11:00 at night on January 2, 2013, and the overwhelming majority of members on the "Image Work" chat group were in favor of releasing an open letter, just to keep up the momentum. The only disagreement was timing: put it out now, or wait? And then Zhang Zhe,

a reporter for the newspaper stationed in Beijing, suggested that journalists stage a walkout. Some agreed, but more were opposed.

The online flood continued to gain intensity, and the number of
Southern Weekly staffers taking part continued to grow as well. In addi-
tion to the five core editors, veteran editors Xiao Hua and Yuan Lei,
who oversaw the economic and cultural desks respectively, also got
involved. They proposed putting out a statement. In these early moments, everyone acted on their own initiative, and the management,
stuck as they were between a rock and hard place, could do nothing but
watch. Deputy editor in chief Chen Mingyang, often referred to jokingly as "the principal," kept himself busy issuing warnings and urging the
young people not to get overly excited: "What are you all hoping to
achieve? Have you thought this through?"

No one, in fact, could answer Chen's question. The flood had come
so fiercely and so suddenly that it was all a bit hard to comprehend.

Early in the morning of January 3, Yang Jibin made a suggestion in
the WeChat group. All staff members in Guangzhou, he said, should
hold a meeting at the paper's offices that afternoon—he used a familiar
metaphor to show his determination: "No matter what happens, I'm
going in to 'beat the empire.' If there's anyone who disagrees, come and
have a duel with me to settle matters."

At least five or six others agreed that it was imperative everyone get
together to decide how best to "beat the empire." This would not be
easy. Qin Xuan had learned that Yang Jian, Guangdong's deputy minister of propaganda, had spoken to people at *Southern Metropolis Daily*.
Yang had passed on a message from Tuo Zhen: he was not to blame; he
had not even set an eye on the New Year's greeting. Furthermore, Tuo
said he would track down whoever had started this rumor—and that
internet police had already determined the initial source of this information, namely netizens by the name of Wang Xing and Xiao Dang. Qin
Xuan started getting nervous and, with his nerves frazzled, started
thinking about how he could "step up" and take responsibility himself.
Qin, who suffers from hypertension, wrote in his journal at the time:

> My heart rate has stayed steadily above ninety beats per minute. My
> mobile is being monitored and I'm waiting for them to come any
> minute. This makes me really anxious and makes me feel unworthy
> of [my wife] Wu Shan. I've decided not to get her involved. But I'm
> more worried that this will be a protracted battle, and that there's

simply no way to cool things down. I had dinner with Yu Chen and some others, but because I couldn't calm myself down I had to go out for a stroll and read anything I could set my eyes on—billboards, advertisements, village regulations—anything to settle myself down. But nothing did any good.

Qin Xuan's heart rate remained elevated for days. He tried to force himself to avoid Weibo and WeChat, but he couldn't. Eventually, he boarded a flight from Lijiang to *Southern Weekly* headquarters with his overworked heart and a solemn sense of mission. With so much on his mind, it was only after he got on the highway heading downtown that he realized he had left his iPad behind on the plane.

News that Tuo Zhen wanted to track down the people who started the "rumor" about him writing the New Year's greeting quickly circulated among the chat groups. The rising tension again prompted calls for swift action, while others called for calm and careful strategizing.

Yuan Lei: If we're holding a sit-in and taking pictures and whatnot, we need to have demands, otherwise we'll all be going our own way and things will get crazy. Cao Junwu, what time are you guys meeting in Guangzhou? We need something concise and to the point about what Tuo Zhen did, and what our demands are.

Yuan Lei: Demands:

1. Allow us to do normal news and investigative reporting within the scope permitted by the Constitution.
2. Remove provincial propaganda examiners from the Southern Media Group system.

Cao Junwu: Yuan Lei, we can't set the bar so high. We don't want to immediately place ourselves in direct opposition to the Party and propaganda officials. That would be exactly what they're hoping for.

Xiao Bei: We can say that propaganda management and news principles need to be respected; and that the political winds since the Eighteenth Party Congress, including "speaking the truth," need to be honored; that reform and opening must be honored, and that criticisms and suggestions must not be silenced.

Cao Junwu: Yeah, that's the right idea.

Cao Junwu then suggested two possible paths: "If we're looking to gain the sympathy and support of the public and then use that to apply pressure, what we need is a letter of protest or a manifesto written according to *Southern Weekly* values. But if our hope is to use our Party's stability preservation mindset, letting those within the system feel that they must yield a bit just to wind things down, then we need to "oppose the corrupt official while defending the emperor."

The second proposal was the more popular.

Everyone was already walking on eggshells. Anxiety was compounded when, at 3:29 p.m. that day, Su Yongtong suddenly shouted, "My Sina Weibo account has been shut down!" Soon, a dozen others shared with surprise that they too had been banned from social media. This development lent a new urgency to the calls for issuing demands. Additional demands forbidding vengeful retaliation and calling for the reinstatement of the staff's Sina Weibo accounts were hastily added to the draft statement in the works.

Cao Junwu put out an urgent call: "Get in touch with any Big Vs [translator's note: "Big Vs" refers to influential figures on Weibo] you know. . . . What bigwigs do you guys know? Get them on the phone and tell them what is happening."

The argument over strategies continued.

Nong Linxia: We shouldn't do interviews with international media.

Yun Chengxi: Once we use overseas media, things will really heat up.

Jiang Nan: Should we stage a walk-out next week? Nothing like that has ever happened in the history of Chinese newspapers. Open letters, however, are pretty predictable.

Cao Junwu: A walk-out is an arrow we should keep drawn on the bow for now—once we strike for real, they'll freak out.

Yang Jibin: We should all be on the same page about how big of a fuss we are going to make, and how we are going to do so. Drastic moves like going on strike, hunger strikes, resignation, that sort of thing, are explosive. They must be handled with extreme care.

Despite such warnings, the bellicosity in the chat groups showed no signs of fading. At that point, the team drafting the official staff statement gradually transformed into a core team handling the situation, along with Yuan Lei, Xiao Hua, and other department directors. Certain decisions required their approval, but this didn't mean that other perspectives could simply be ignored.

In January 2013, WeChat was a new interactive messaging service, created less than two years earlier. It had only been widely and regularly used for a year or so. Yet it is impossible to imagine the *Southern Weekly* affair having unfolded the way it did without WeChat.

"WeChat made it possible to essentially have twenty-four-hour round-the-clock meetings, even when we were all in different places, breaking through limitations in space and time. Smartphones, meanwhile, brought together virtual space and the real world." These were Qin Xuan's reflections on new technology's role in this affair. "These tools are extremely important for social movements."

Offline, strategic discussions more limited in scope were also happening around dinner tables. On the afternoon of January 4, in a restaurant called Be There or Be Square, a group of journalists from the *Southern Weekly* Beijing bureau discussed a resolution that was posted soon thereafter to the WeChat group. In Shanghai too, editorial staff members met over lunch. That night in Panyu, Shi Zhe, Yang Jibin, Cao Junwu, and Su Yongtong went out for roast lamb. Yang Jibin later summed up the discussion that evening as follows: "the consensus we reached was to take lessons from the events of 1989, never underestimating the fundamental hostility of the system."

But outraged staffers were not the only people arranging dinner meetings. On the afternoon of January 3, a few senior editors of the newspaper received a text message from the paper's deputy general manager, Wu Chuanzhen: that night, he and Chief Hui (meaning Wang Genghui, the Southern Media Group deputy editor in chief in charge of *Southern Weekly*) and Chief Can (meaning Huang Can) wanted to invite everyone out for a New Year's dinner.

What was the purpose of this dinner, they wondered: To feel them out? To placate them? To trap them? Everyone made their guesses in the WeChat group, and news of the dinner gradually became public knowledge. It would soon become apparent just how difficult it was to maintain barriers between the seemingly private forums of WeChat and the very public forum of Weibo.

Instant communication technologies seem to have accelerated the speed of the movement. Right before the New Year's dinner, the *Southern Weekly* staff issued their first public statement via Weibo. As they knew their statement could not represent the paper in any official capacity, they provisionally registered a Weibo ID called @Southern-WeeklyEditorialDivision. Cao Junwu soon discovered that in their urgency they had written the year as 2012 rather than 2013. It was, after all, only early January.

Ersha Island, where the dinner was held, is a long and narrow island in the middle of the Pearl River, on the southern end of Guangzhou's central business district. It is a space of quiet amid the bustling city, with garden restaurants serving mostly local Cantonese cuisine. While the dishes that night tasted fine, the gathering itself was a bit off.

Wu Chuanzhen took the lead during the first half of the dinner. A former editor at *Southern Weekly*, Wu had done well for himself since joining the business side of the paper. He had in particular brought in tens of millions in revenue beyond traditional advertising sources. Wu seemed to have come with a mission that night. He talked about *Southern Weekly*'s vision—for example, how it would expand into multiple formats, how the employees of the newspaper would have rich opportunities for career development, with prospects for endless returns. Huang Can and Wang Genghui would toss in their two cents from time to time, largely along the same lines.

Enough was spent on that dinner, the editors later said, to solve world hunger—but Yang Jibin couldn't work up an appetite. The editors wanted to bring the conversation back to the issue of the New Year's special edition and the ensuing storm. But their desire was not reciprocated.

The newspaper's photo editor, Feng Fei, recounted an interesting detail from the meal. He had spotted Huang Can, who supposedly never used Weibo, quietly scrolling through Weibo on his phone at one point that evening. Feng Fei really wanted to catch a glimpse of his Weibo pseudonym but couldn't quite make it out.

As the evening wound down, the deputy editors in chief Chen Ming-yang and Wu Xiaofeng couldn't stop themselves from raising the issue of the New Year's edition. Considering the ill will that had built up recently at the newspaper, they said, there had to be a change in the management methods. Wang Genghui and Huang Can did not respond.

Everyone left that evening with a bad taste in his mouth.

The storm over the New Year's edition continued to grow online. At noon on January 4, a group of former *Southern Weekly* editors and journalists sent out an open letter on Sina Weibo with thirty-five signatures. This was the earliest expression of outside support. This open letter stated that "Tuo Zhen ordered numerous changes and deletions to the New Year's special edition, resulting in numerous errors." "Tuo Zhen's actions," it added, "were out of bounds, unauthorized, ignorant, and completely unnecessary." Clearly, the letter said, Tuo Zhen must accept blame, resign, and issue a public apology. The letter included passages that gave direct voice to the outrage so many felt about this incident:

> We believe this is an age that requires hope, yet he hollows out hope; this is an age that yearns for equality, yet he stands arrogantly above all others; this is an age of growing open-mindedness, yet his actions are closed-minded and thoughtless; this is an age that celebrates learning, yet he is crude and foolish. . . .
>
> As former staffers at *Southern Weekly*, we love this paper. For many years, it has survived amid great challenges—it is not easy to build and maintain a top-quality paper. We have been happy to see her grow up in the warm and open earth of southern Guangdong, loved and protected by people both inside and outside the system. The newspaper has had its moments of misfortune and of glory. It has been labeled all types of things, but we know very well that a group of idealistic youth is gathered there, even today when having "ideals" is openly mocked by so many. In essence, this idealism is the hope that our country can become a better place, that the people of our country can live better lives. History can attest, and will continue to attest, to the sincerity of these hopes.

The same day, open letters from former *Southern Weekly* interns, and from colleagues from other publications housed at 289 Guangzhou Avenue, also went public via Weibo.

Moved by these shows of solidarity, the staffers at *Southern Weekly* reflected on and discussed the role their own statement could play. Zhang Zhe offered his view: "These open letters give us some time to figure things out. We can figure out how to deal with both the provincial government and the central leadership . . . if the central leadership is unhappy with the thoughtless destruction of this new open environment in which everyone has invested so much energy, this could work to our advantage."

Yang Jibin also felt that momentum would continue to be strong. He wrote: "I estimate that from this afternoon, the pressure of public opinion will gradually begin to be directed at us, urging us to take action. They need their heroes. But we must stay clearheaded. Of course, we can't abandon the possibility of resignation, hunger strikes, or other such methods. But we can't speak of these things so cavalierly. We'll try to get our statement finished today, but we mustn't get too hotheaded."

Opinions flew back and forth on the WeChat group, careening from topic to topic, and there was always a fear whenever you stepped away that you were about to miss something crucial—so you would spend all your downtime scrolling back through to see what people had said and what you had missed.

Just after 2:00 p.m. on January 4, supporters of the two factions—advocates of urgency and caution, respectively—again fought it out in the WeChat group:

Hong De: Now that the elders [meaning former *Southern Weekly* colleagues] have put out their open letter, we must follow up quickly with our own. The more we wait the less effect it will have, and the more we will look passive. We can't delay any longer.

Yuan Lei: There's no need to be so eager. Right now the information we have from various quarters is cause for optimism. . . . Just so long as we keep our target focused . . . this is from people close to Liu Yunshan and Xi Jinping.

Next, people shared their thoughts on what the demands in the open letter should be:

Cao Junwu: My thoughts are as follows:

1. The meeting scheduled for the seventh should remain unchanged.
2. The open letter from our old colleagues is great. They are helping us in the best way they can, not engaging in a writing contest with us. I don't see how it would show passiveness on our part to not release a letter immediately.
3. In the wake of the open letter from our former colleagues, our task is to be clearer about our demands, not to fire off accusations—particularly, we need to get specific about our demands.
4. Our demands are basically of two kinds, the broader demand of being allowed the right to report on the news normally, and the more focused, internal demand that an editorial committee be established that has a real grasp of editorial procedures and the limits of management. As to whether we raise the issue of Tuo Zhen or even push for his resignation, that is open to discussion.
5. As things appear at the moment, there is still plenty of public pressure and attention, in particular after the letter from *Southern Weekly* veterans, so holding things together until the seventh isn't a problem. This is also a great opportunity for us to take a deep breath and watch how things develop.
6. We need to immediately discuss our concrete demands and draft an action plan.

Xia Tangxi: We must force Tuo Zhen out, otherwise it's meaningless, and things can go right back to how they were in no time.

Guang Yuan: Given the situation, we must reveal Tuo Zhen for what he is; otherwise the days ahead will be dark for *Southern Weekly*.

Xiao Bei: Directly toppling Tuo Zhen would be difficult. At the most, he might be quietly transferred.

Xia Tangxi: If we never even raise the idea of getting rid of him, it wouldn't just be difficult; it would be impossible.

Cao Junwu: We will:

1. Jointly raise the issue of holding a general editorial committee meeting on January 7 (but this must be decided by the sixth, so that those who live outside the city can get here on time).
2. Discuss our concrete demands (at the latest, we'll have the results of that discussion tomorrow, as well as a decision on whether we should first put out a statement for discussion).
3. In order to facilitate communication with the government, we won't elevate the discussion to such sensitive matters as freedom and democracy. The above are the results of our meeting.

Inside the WeChat group you could witness *Southern Weekly* values in practice: values such as equality, tolerance, and freedom, the very things staffers new and old treasured about this paper. But from another angle, these values could also lead to rootless indecision. This was particularly true in moments like this when time was of the essence and clear direction was needed. While no one had a problem getting worked up in the WeChat group, the result was a swirling pot of emotion with no clear path forward emerging. After a few days, everyone who posted a comment seemed like a commander who nevertheless couldn't rally an army behind him. Everyone eventually started to feel a bit hopeless.

Reflecting upon these events, many people expressed their regrets at the staff's hesitation and weakness. Such regrets, however, were not new. People were already saying similar things when I had just arrived at the newspaper back in 2003.

Southern Weekly intern Shao Shiwei was on New Year's vacation in Hong Kong at the time. When he saw the storm over the New Year's special edition growing, he was confident that the paper's editors would take decisive action. He hurried back to Guangzhou to provide support. Upon his return he was shocked to find the editorial department at *Southern Weekly* entirely empty, without a soul in sight. All that Shao Shiwei could do was to write and pass along Weibo posts supporting *Southern Weekly*. He posted and posted, re-posted and re-posted. Here at the heart of the storm, the only sound he could hear was the "whisk" of Weibo posts as they zipped from his desktop into cyberspace.

Early in the morning of January 5, Yang Jibin sat down and began to write a public statement representing the paper's staff. His idea was to follow the example of Li Datong in the *"Freezing Point* Incident." For readers who are unfamiliar with these events, in January 2006, the *Freezing Point* supplement of *China Youth Daily* was suspended for publishing an essay by historian Yuan Weishi criticizing perverse historical representations of the violently xenophobic Boxer Rebellion as "patriotic." The official News Commentary Group severely criticized the essay. The editor of the supplement, Li Datong, planned to make an appeal to the Central Discipline Inspection Commission as a member of the Communist Party, explaining how the propaganda department had violated organizational procedures. The letter Li had penned was framed in Party-speak and made a particular effort to make demands that were feasible within the constraints of the system. In Li's case, however, the Central Discipline Inspection Commission did not accept the letter, raising questions about whether this was indeed the wisest course of action.

Accordingly, disagreements persisted regarding how best to proceed. The vast majority of the staff called for a statement to be issued as quickly as possible, but the editors were in favor of using it as their trump card. Chen Mingyang was not in favor of writing at all and hoped that any such public statement would focus only on the immediate matter at hand, the New Year's special edition—because, as Chen said, the Party would undoubtedly resist discussing anything beyond this. Yang Jibin pointed out, however, that young people at *Southern Weekly* felt exactly the opposite way: everything needed to be on the table in order to exert maximum pressure.

Procrastination and dispute meant that this statement took much longer to be sent than it should have. But eventually, this tardiness had unexpectedly fantastic results.

While Yang Jibin was sitting down to write this public statement, Cao Junwu was also writing a position statement. All morning on January 5, the WeChat group was filled with calls to hurry up and do something. Then, close to 11:00 in the morning, there was an answer:

Yuan Lei: Yesterday we stayed up late talking, and finally reached a basic consensus:

1. We will draft and release a second public statement today;

2. We will work hard to ensure that the general editorial committee meeting we applied for yesterday is held on the sixth;

3. Due to time restrictions, as well as our plan to save some "artillery" for later, the statement we will release today will be fairly concise, and our next step will be discussed and decided collectively at the general editorial committee meeting;

4. We will welcome comments on and revisions, because, after all, this statement should represent everyone and we don't want it to have any negative impact;

5. We advocate democracy, and we are practicing democracy.

Once a draft is ready, we will post it for everyone. The phone calls yesterday were endless. Some were encouraging, others said we're too soft, that we don't have the courage to do this or that. I am sure many of us are receiving many calls of this kind. When I get these calls, I always remind them that any war is about strategy. Please be assured that we are not going soft.

The matter of how to sign this second statement somehow grew into a point of contention. Before the real challenges, divisions, and choices arrived, everyone was able to linger on some considerably less significant questions.

Yu Dongxi: We must each sign it ourselves. The objective of terror is precisely to make each of us want to hide and cover our faces. What we need is each specific individual's name. We don't need to be too worried about efficiency so much—after all, how many of us are there? Not that many. We just need someone to be responsible for head-counting. I'm sure most people will agree to have their names added. It won't be much of an issue keeping track of everyone.

Bao Gang: Democracy is the natural enemy of efficiency. I'll handle all the editing myself.

Nan An: Coercion is no good.

Chang Gang: If it belongs to all of us but our personal opinions don't figure into it, then that's certainly more efficient, but then how are we any different from Tuo Zhen?

Dong Xiaonan: If just one of us disagrees, then it can't be said to be written by all of us, no?

Cao Junwu: It'll be from the editorial department then, that way everyone doesn't have to sign it.

Tianhe Bei: Not everyone in the editorial department agrees.

Dong Hu: Make it from the editorial department, not from each one of us, one by one. Let's not drag this out too long.

As this argument proceeded, everyone who spoke with *Southern Weekly* staff had just one question: When will you be issuing a public statement? Clearly, it was no longer a secret that something was brewing inside the paper. There were also hints that even Huang Can knew about some of the plans. Inside the chat group, suspicions began to emerge—was someone sharing information beyond the group? Was this forum still secure?

On the afternoon of January 5, Yang Jibin and Chu Zhaoxin had a public dispute online.

Chu Zhaoxin: Colleagues at *Southern Metropolis Daily*, *Southern Metropolis Weekly*, and *Southern People Weekly* have all signed statements directly criticizing Tuo Zhen. And damnit, here we are still talking about so-called strategy.

Yang Jibin: Brothers, there is never any shame in talking about strategy.

Chu Zhaoxin: It's precisely too much "strategy" that has brought *Southern Weekly* to where it is today.

Yang Jibin: Too much strategy is always better than no strategy at all. Chaoxin, we need to have clear heads. Especially right now. . . .

I don't have a problem with any individual saying whatever they please, but when it comes to using these two words, *Southern Weekly*, to make our views known, we must be as careful as careful can be. This isn't about lacking courage—if it were courage that we lacked we would have never come to this point in the first place. It's about being responsible to this paper. We don't have the right to sacrifice *Southern Weekly* to our impulses. . . .

You must know what a twisted system we face. We need to be cool-headed and rational because just as we force the other side to step back, we don't want to create an opportunity for them to lean in and finish off *Southern Weekly*, which is exactly what they want to do. They can get rid of Yang Jibin, get rid of Su Yongtong or Cao Junwu, but we can't give them a pretext to get rid of *Southern Weekly* altogether. . . .

The real lesson of June 4th is not that we need to be more persistent or more courageous. The real lesson of June 4th is that we can't piss off people in the system.

Chu Zhaoxin:

1. *Southern Weekly* is where it is today not for lack of rationality, but rather due to too much "rationality."
2. Likeminded publications have all voiced their support, but we are still worrying about whether revenge will be exacted and using the *Southern Weekly* name to shield ourselves. Is this rational?
3. We should sign our names.

Yang Jibin: No one has ever been opposed to signing our names, dammit. This isn't the time for a courage contest. . . . Where were you when we were in the office starting all this up? Fuck, some people can't resist engaging in friendly fire. . . .

What do you mean by saying *Southern Weekly* is where it is today not for lack of rationality, but rather due to too much rationality? If we reject reason, what do we have left?

Chu Zhaoxin: I had a few phone calls just now. Thanks everyone. Scores of our colleagues from *Southern Metropolis Daily*, *Southern People Weekly*, and *Southern Metropolis Weekly* have pointed the finger directly at Tuo Zhen on Weibo. They've taken on great risk in doing so. Out of a sense of moral responsibility, we should sign our names individually to stand together with them.

The exchange between Yang Jibin and Chu Zhaoxin continued, neither able to be swayed by the other.

Born in the Shaanxi countryside, Yang Jibin had a complex personality. He could have quite a temper at times, but he could also be cool as ice at critical moments. "Among all of us, I played the *Empire* the best," he commented. His strength, he felt, was that he had a head for strategizing, and he could apply this expertise in his everyday struggles.

> I often draw analogies to video games. For example, if you aren't yet 100 percent sure, then don't even think about engaging in battle. When you're playing with the real experts, we know that two armies must retreat immediately after they encounter each other. Rookies will just stand there and try to fight it out. Age of Empires is a multilayered game. At any moment, you must keep in mind what the most important task you are facing is: mobilize the right people for the task you are addressing and let everyone else take a rest.

Shi Zhe perhaps had more distance from the spiraling crisis at *Southern Weekly* than Yang Jibin. He did what he had to do, but throughout the affair he saw himself more as an outside observer, watching developments from a distance, as if it were a game that someone else was playing. He laughed as he recalled the atmosphere inside the paper: "Everyone was showing off, thinking they were more important than everyone else."

Then, just as the first statement from the editors had been sent out right before the New Year's dinner on Ersha Island, so the second statement was finally issued just ahead of the editorial board meeting. The statement, "To Our Readers and Everyone Who Cares About *Southern Weekly*," read as follows:

> Dearest readers, esteemed media colleagues, and everyone who cares about *Southern Weekly*:

We express our thanks to all of you! It's only because of you that we are still standing. We have written before that "Together, we are like beams of light wrapped around one another." We have said that "one word of truth is of greater gravity than this entire world."

Three days ago, we spoke the truth, and your voices have affirmed the truth of what we say. This is the greatest reward we can ever hope for.

Two days ago, we released a statement calling for a full investigation into this matter. But two days have now passed, and the truth is no clearer now than before, as ever more people demanding to know the truth are being silenced.

We hope that an authoritative special investigation group can be formed, enabling the truth to see the light of day. The incident three days ago only served to ignite long-smoldering embers. According to our statistics, which are not necessarily complete, a total of 1,034 articles were altered or altogether removed at *Southern Weekly* in 2012. Over the past year, we have faced a relentless regime of irrational censorship: extensive revisions, cutting reports, killing entire editions.

We don't fear causing offense. We believe this is a matter of the most basic principles of journalism. It is because the problem is so intrinsic to everything that we do that we must say directly what we feel. We don't take these actions out of anger, but rather out of a necessary sense of human dignity, accountability, and honor.

There is nothing that we fear losing, apart from our own souls and the trust all of you place in us. We don't expect to win anything apart from demonstrating our clear consciences, and a chance to continue demonstrating that to all of you.

We trust in hope, rather than choosing fear.

Our demands:

1. The establishment of a sufficiently credible special investigation team to thoroughly examine the New Year's Edition process and the reasons behind this entire affair, with full public disclosure of its findings.
2. The full reinstatement of all social media accounts that have been closed as a result of discussing this incident.
3. We ask that no one who has discussed or participated in this incident be attacked or restricted in any way, or by any means.
4. We reserve the right to continue taking action.

Southern Weekly editorial team, January 5, 2013, 14:10

Once this second statement was released, several people both inside and outside the newspaper felt that its tone was far too restrained. Opinions were highly polarized.

Xi Wan: Colleagues, I really cannot accept this. If we can't pull together, I'll just announce my own intent to go on strike. And I encourage my colleagues to support me.

Xi Wan: I'm not saying this to throw cold water on everyone. Truly. But so many people in the group have stuck out their necks in signing in support of us and run the risk of being disciplined. They hope to see us take some real action as well, even if that means being tougher in our demands.

Shuang Qiao: It's OK to be a little more reserved, I think.

Tong Jiheng: I don't think striking on your own, making yourself into a martyr, is going to do much good. What is most important here is public attention and support. Our colleagues in the media can do as they please, but we should proceed more cautiously.

Yuan Lei: No striking yet. Let's everyone list our demands tonight.

Nan An: Striking means leaving our positions—they'll be glad to be rid of us.

Shang Xia Jiu: We don't necessarily need to go on strike, but our position can be a bit firmer.

Shuang Qiao: If even we don't know what we are doing, we have no chance of standing up to them. Game over.

Xi Wan: We can struggle against them strategically. But what exactly is our strategy? What is our probable course of action here?

Yang Jibin: We have no strategy. Because no one planned this in advance. But we have some principles—at the end of the day, this is like a card game. We look at what cards come up, and then play from our deck accordingly. And we definitely need to save our strongest suit for last. Sit-ins, resignation—those are our strongest cards. Our kings and aces. . . .

I don't know how it's going to play out. Because I've never done this before. But that's not an issue. All we need to remember is what we really want. And what we want right now is something that we can get through more moderate means of opposition. We're not out to plunder but rather to claim what is rightfully ours.

5

TUO ZHEN DID IT (?)

Wu Wei, who oversaw social media management at *Southern Weekly*, was added to the chat group on the afternoon of January 4. His first impression was that things inside weren't quite right: most people seemed to have already decided beyond a doubt that it was Tuo Zhen himself who had altered the New Year's greeting. Were they not aware that Huang Can had denied this? Even if they had no reason to believe Huang Can, what evidence did they actually have to prove this was all Tuo Zhen's fault?

On the night that news of the special edition's changes had blown up on Weibo, Wu Wei had fired a text message to Cao Junwu to get a clearer picture of what exactly had happened. "Did he really write this text himself?" he had asked. The answer: "Exactly who wrote it we still don't know. But this stuff wasn't originally on the front page, and he definitely changed the New Year's greeting himself. I don't know how exactly these changes were made, but Huang Can did not notify any of us editors."

Some time after that, Huang Can called Wu Wei. The editor in chief was explicit: "the preface was written by our own people, written by Wu Xiaofeng, and the text message [to that effect] is still in my mobile phone."

On the morning of January 6, Singapore's *Lianhe Zaobao* ran a report on its website to this effect:

> Concerning the incident in which the Guangdong Provincial Propaganda Department is accused of altering the New Year's greeting at

Southern Weekly, an official source familiar with the matter reveals that Tuo Zhen, minister of the Guangdong Provincial Propaganda Department, was not in Guangdong at the time, and the matter has nothing to do with him or with the Provincial Propaganda Department.

As to who altered the New Year's greeting at *Southern Weekly*, the source provided no further explanation.

The online uproar over Tuo Zhen had gone on for three days and four nights. Was it all completely fabricated? There were those who firmly believed it, and others who doubted it. But in any case, the issue was explosive. Ever more people were drawn into the mystery of what exactly Tuo had or had not done.

Where had this idea that "Tuo Zhen did it" come from in the first place?

Qin Xuan's diary provides a glimpse into how this idea first emerged:

Night of January 2, 2013—When we reached the restaurant, I think it was Yu Chen and others who asked if this was true [about Tuo Zhen]. I remember giving Shi Zhe a call, but he didn't answer. So, I called Cao Junwu. There were lots of people around me at the time.

Cao Junwu told me on the phone that it was true, and that there were witnesses. I remember asking whether "he," meaning Tuo Zhen, had gone to the proof room himself and made these changes. Later, I couldn't confirm any of this with Cao Junwu, and he said he didn't remember me calling. It could have been a misunderstanding. Maybe he was thinking about Huang Can, while I was thinking about Tuo Zhen. Now it's hard to say for sure.

There are discrepancies between Qin Xuan's, Cao Junwu's, and Shi Zhe's recollections of this exchange. When I spoke to Shi Zhe about this, his first response was that he didn't remember any calls, but later he said that maybe he did receive a call from Qin Xuan. "I remember saying that there was no way to be certain. And I had no idea that he planned to make such claims public."

Cao Junwu is adamant that he doesn't remember receiving a call from Qin Xuan.

Qin Xuan is also adamant that he never told Cao that he intended to release the news on his own Weibo account. "I just wanted to get it out," he said. "That was my decision. It had nothing to do with him."

Looking back, Shi Zhe feels that the spread of such uncorroborated information about Tuo Zhen was part and parcel of the workplace culture at *Southern Weekly*. "We routinely decided that any abnormal controls [on our content] had been done by Tuo Zhen. Either Tuo or the Provincial Propaganda Department. It was probably our casual approach to these types of claims that led to inaccurate leaks."

There certainly was not enough evidence to say that "Tuo Zhen did it." And according to propaganda department insiders, Tuo saw this as a malicious attempt to smear him. At the same time, it was also a massive oversimplification of the entire matter. What we see in the rumors of Tuo Zhen's involvement in the New Year's special edition is, from beginning to end, a misunderstanding produced by a chemical reaction of explosive anger and inaccurate claims. The experience of the previous seven months, in which editors and journalists had been subjected to unprecedented levels of censorship, had deeply embittered many at *Southern Weekly*; basically, at this point there was scarcely anything that they couldn't imagine Tuo Zhen doing.

"He reminded me of that inspector in *Les Misérables*, the one who's out to kill Jean Valjean," said one commercial media boss who attended a meeting between Tuo Zhen and local media chiefs shortly after the new minister arrived in Guangdong in May 2012. In the months that followed, all of the media bosses at the meeting found themselves hounded like Jean Valjean by their new propaganda czar.

In the early 1980s, as Guangdong was the first place in China to implement reform and opening, new innovations had emerged one after another from this province's rich and fertile soil. *Southern Weekly* was what is known as a "child paper," born in 1984 as a spin-off of the Party's provincial-level mouthpiece, *Nanfang Daily*. Despite its official links, from the start its founders hoped to leave behind the old Soviet-style propaganda newspaper model that *Nanfang Daily* represented. They wanted their publication to speak for the people rather than simply serve as a propaganda tool. Such a paper, they felt, could nurture new ideas within the old authoritarian system. Their founding principle was based in a daring compromise: "There may be truths of which we cannot speak, but we must not speak falsehoods." It was a risky path destined to win allies in the emerging new marketplace, but also sparking resistance from the state's media minders.

At its peak, *Southern Weekly's* daily circulation reached more than one million copies. The market rewarded the newspaper for its courage. By the year 2000, annual salaries at the paper were among the highest in the industry, averaging around 200,000 yuan.

By the 1990s many other commercial media in China had followed *Southern Weekly's* lead, but *Southern Weekly* remained the flag bearer for a new sort of newspaper, always pushing the boundaries to cover the important stories and issues of the day, and thereby selling papers— even as political controls on the media remained unexpectedly resilient.

By the turn of the century, however, *Southern Weekly* was the target of unrelenting pressure from the authorities. Editors at all levels were removed and replaced one after another. Then, in 2003, Zhang Dong-ming, the former director of news media at the Guangdong Propaganda Department, was named editor in chief, for the purpose of controlling this perpetually "unruly" paper. Having benefited greatly from a policy of opening, *Southern Weekly* suddenly found itself trapped in an increasingly stifling environment.

Although *Southern Weekly* never quite recaptured the influence that it had at its pre-2003 peak, it nevertheless remained an important political symbol in reform-era China. When US president Barack Obama and German chancellor Angela Merkel visited China, both offered the paper exclusive interviews. Such offers made the authorities not only nervous but also a bit embarrassed; visiting heads of state had explicitly chosen not to speak with state media. The hotel where Merkel stayed was just a little over a kilometer away from No. 289, but in the end her interview was canceled due to various forms of pressure. Although Obama's interview was completed and published, it was nevertheless complicated at every step by the propaganda authorities. *Southern Weekly's* relationship with "foreign powers" clearly made the authorities very anxious.

In 2009, Huang Can, who had worked for years at the provincial party mouthpiece *Nanfang Daily*, was appointed editor in chief of *Southern Weekly*. Huang had been working with the Southern Media Group since graduating from university in the 1980s, so he should have understood the paper's culture. Yet once he took control, his approach immediately clashed with this culture. Editors and writers sometimes had the feeling that Huang's censorship was even more aggressive than the propaganda department's.

Southern Weekly was already suffering under Huang Can's editor-
ship when Tuo Zhen's arrival in Guangdong in 2012 further exacerbated matters. The Southern Media Group had produced several of the
country's most outspoken newspapers, including *Southern Weekly*,
Southern Metropolis Daily, and *Southern People Weekly*, and many
observers guessed that Tuo Zhen had arrived intending to clean house.
Never before had a senior propaganda official been so suddenly air-
lifted into Guangdong.

"The propaganda battlefield has been entrusted to us by the Party. It
is our responsibility to hold our ground. If we lose even an inch, then
we must win it back." These words, secretly recorded by one media
executive, were the first words Tuo Zhen addressed to media bosses in
Guangdong after his arrival. Clearly, he had come with a mission. At-
tendees at this first meeting remember Tuo Zhen introducing himself
as follows: "At newspapers under my watch, not a single word is published before I've had a chance to examine it." He urged all the media
bosses present to emulate his style, leaving nothing beyond their grasp.
One media boss who was present laughed as he recalled this moment:
"what a sick way of thinking."

Some scholars have called *Southern Weekly* the spiritual homeland
of China's liberal camp. Tuo Zhen's objective, it seemed, was to destroy
this homeland and all that it represented. Almost immediately, Tuo sent
out a new directive from his command center: all news pitches were to
be reported to him first, and none could be pursued until he had given
the go-ahead. After layouts were completed for the newspapers, they
were to be sent to a designated mailbox of the propaganda department
in PDF format. Nothing could go to press before he had given the
green light. This level of proactive censorship was essentially unprecedented, showing just how eager Tuo was to "hold our ground," as he
had said. Control in the past had largely been exercised through directives, usually delivered by phone, with no written record. Official lines
were never drawn all that clearly, but media that dared to transgress
them too obviously would be disciplined. Despite its obvious constraints, this was still a primarily reactive censorship system, outlined
clearly in China's 2005 Regulations for Administration of Newspaper
Publications.

But with the arrival of Tuo Zhen, management switched from a
reactive to a proactive mode of media management. "It was no longer

just a question of pushing us around," said one deputy editor at *Southern Weekly* of the time after Tuo Zhen's arrival. "They had us by the balls." Ye Weimin recalls with some regret that the staff at *Southern Weekly* didn't sufficiently recognize the threat posed by Tuo Zhen. They believed that Wang Yang, the province's top Party leader at the time, was taking steps toward further reform and was likely to protect *Southern Weekly*. Only later, when things grew substantially worse, did they realize how naïve they had been.

Southern Weekly staff could not for the moment provide any evidence to counter *Lianhe Zaobao*'s version of events claiming that Tuo Zhen was not involved in the changes. Internally, some staff members felt that no one at *Southern Weekly* had ever actually said that it was Tuo Zhen who had altered the New Year's greeting, and they shouldn't be held responsible for the rumors flying around on the internet. So why should they be obliged to clarify matters?

Others felt that these unconfirmed rumors were a real problem. But they also leaned more toward keeping quiet on these matters. They feared shifts in public opinion, a quagmire of explanations and counter-explanations, and the possibility that these rumors could provide a pretext for the Provincial Propaganda Department to seek revenge. There was also perhaps an undeniable emotional element to this silence—who wouldn't want to see Tuo Zhen ridiculed and forced to take responsibility for all he had done? What point was there in clearing his name? He had, after all, created the environment in which such abuses could take place.

At the same time, however, it really was not possible to maintain silence. The online furor over the New Year's special edition had grown much louder than anyone had expected. And there were many people at *Southern Weekly* and others with a close connection to the paper who wanted to take advantage of the lack of clarity about who exactly was involved to pressure both Tuo Zhen and Huang Can to step down.

Most people didn't want to see Tuo Zhen emerge from this incident unscathed. There was, however, one notable exception: Huang Can. Soon after the incident occurred, Huang had gone to extraordinary lengths to keep propaganda officials from being implicated in this affair. He quietly registered his own brand-new Weibo account called "No Regrets at *Southern Weekly*." He wrote three posts that he sent to Wu Wei as text messages before posting them to his new Weibo account:

"How could a propaganda minister write those sentences himself?"

(January 3, 17:20, Sina Weibo)

"Don't believe those making wild guesses on Weibo. Those sentences were written by the editors themselves."

(January 3, 16:58, Sina Weibo)

"I've seen everyone debating the New Year's greeting at *Southern Weekly*, and some are really worked up. But based on what I know, the New Year's greeting in this edition of *Southern Weekly* was drafted collaboratively by the paper's editors, and this paper's senior figures signed off on it, only making partial changes. It's not anything like what people are saying!"

(January 3, 02:16, Sina Weibo)

Never clarifying who was behind the account or why they were qualified to comment, "No Regrets at *Southern Weekly*" had no impact whatsoever: there were no comments on the posts and no shares. The account was like a small stone tossed into raging waters. No one noticed, except perhaps their intended audience: Huang Can's superiors.

6

CAN YOU KNOW WHAT
YOU DON'T KNOW?

"**I**'ve checked back through our posts on Weibo at the time. On public forums, we stuck to our journalistic ethics, never directly pointing the finger at Tuo Zhen. . . . Without evidence, we couldn't just openly make such claims." As Cao Junwu sits at home, recollecting the events of 2013, every word seems to echo through the bare space of his living room, which is curiously devoid of furniture. "In the beginning we didn't think much of it. In private conversation, of course we pointed our fingers at Tuo."

As this incident gathered steam, the line between private and public spaces grew increasingly unclear, producing new problems.

On the morning of January 5, former *Southern Weekly* reporter Nan Xianghong received a call from veteran magazine editor Hu Shuli. In rapid bursts of speech, Hu claimed she had learned that the changes to the New Year's edition were done neither by propaganda officials nor specifically Tuo Zhen, but rather by staff inside *Southern Weekly*. It could have been Huang Can or Wu Xiaofeng, but this was still unclear. Hu exhorted Nan to explain to her former colleagues the importance of getting their facts straight.

Hu, the founder of two of China's most respected and influential news media, *Caijing* magazine and Caixin Media, was a figure of immense authority in Chinese media who also had close and lasting contacts with senior leaders. Hu Shuli explained to Nan Xianghong that her words of advice came from certain "powers," most likely meaning a certain high-level leader. Hu cautioned that if a mistaken narrative spread too far it could be extremely detrimental to *Southern Weekly*, so she advised getting to the bottom of this matter as quickly as possible and adjusting strategy accordingly.

Thirty minutes later, Nan Xianghong's phone rang again. This time Hu Shuli told her that she could confirm that the preface had been requested by Tuo Zhen and written by Wu Xiaofeng. She hoped that the staff at *Southern Weekly* would recognize that people inside the paper, rather than just Tuo Zhen, also bore some responsibility.

When the staff at *Southern Weekly* learned of Hu Shuli's comments, some were unhappy. They interpreted her emphasis on "internal responsibility" as an attempt to exonerate state propaganda officials.

But it wasn't just Hu Shuli who was digging into the truth behind this incident. As rumors flew, many people who understood the workings of the media and officials' work roles therein wondered: How could Tuo Zhen just roll up his sleeves and get involved in writing copy? And how could he be going personally to the newsroom and getting so intimately involved in production?

In this vacuum of uncertainty, chaos grew inside *Southern Weekly*. Some made their own inquiries. Some called for a full investigation. Others withdrew altogether from the discussion. And still others grew impatient. The arguing and apprehension over what had actually happened vexed everyone, to the point that one editor called the issue "a painful, itching pustule."

"We were definitely anxious and scared. If it turned out that it really was Huang Can and Wu Xiaofeng, then the joke was on us. Even though we weren't the ones spreading rumors about Tuo Zhen, the rest of the world would assume we were the source." Cao Junwu confesses that he became extremely agitated whenever someone questioned claims of Tuo Zhen's responsibility. At least two editors of the special edition lost control during an internal staff meeting: "Will everyone stop pretending they don't know what is going on!" They all knew just how long the long arm of the propaganda department was. But at the same time, this wasn't necessarily proof.

As early as noon on January 4, at the gathering at the Be There or Be Square restaurant, Beijing staff members had felt that the basic facts about the changes were unclear. By around 4:00 p.m. that afternoon, Zhang Zhe shared their thoughts with the WeChat group, calling for a detailed investigation into what had happened, regardless of who was responsible:

1. There must be an investigation into the New Year's issue. If errors about Yu the Great were not the doing of propaganda officials, then it must be made clear who is responsible. If the people responsible are internal staff members then they should be stripped of their credentials, apologize publicly, and resign.
2. A general editorial board meeting should be held before January 6 to discuss the major editorial incidents of the past year. That meeting should be attended by representatives from each desk, with full minutes of the meeting published on the internal server.
3. The content of the killed articles from the New Year's special edition should be made available and the reasons for censoring them fully explained. An internal system should be established whereby cut articles can be displayed on the internal server, and in the future, all killed articles, the person responsible for the decision, and the reasons for their decision should be made available.
4. We should demand that an "Investigative Report into the 2013 New Year's Special Edition" be submitted to the provincial Party leadership and the propaganda department in the newspaper's name, and that there be an inquiry into the responsibility borne by the propaganda department.

This was the first and only time the members of the Beijing bureau, accounting for half of the paper's editorial staff, offered their views. After this, they gradually fell silent—partly because they worried that the information they had was inaccurate, and partly because they wanted to maintain internal unity.

Cao Junwu immediately voiced his objections, not holding back in the slightest:

> There are problems straightaway from the first point. Damnit, of course this is the work of the Provincial Propaganda Department! This has built up to this point, if we now make it all about internal management, the damn provincial propaganda authorities will only become ever more powerful. I am confident that some people lower on the totem pole will be happy to take the blame for their superiors.

But what after all would be the point of just taking down Huang Can?

That afternoon, Wu Wei, who had just been brought into the WeChat group, watched as things started to boil over, with everyone engaged in back-and-forth on that one all-too-familiar question:

Nan An: The key question is whether the provincial propaganda department instigated this. If we say they did, we need to provide evidence.

Tian Xin Xi: I suggest we look for eyewitnesses to get to the bottom of Tuo Zhen's visit to the proof room on January 2. Right now, we don't have any firm evidence.

Si You Xin: Regardless of whether it was Tuo Zhen, he is the one we must go after.

Nong Lin Xia: Huang Can called me to make three points:

1. The bit on the front page about Yu the Great taming the floods wasn't written by Tuo, but by someone at the paper. They were under so much pressure that they made mistakes. In order to "protect" that person, he can't say who it was.
2. The New Year's greeting was largely changed internally, with only a few changes from the propaganda department.
3. Articles were removed from the special edition because the topics were too niche, lacking coherence. Huang says it's fine to share his post.

Kang Wang Bei: Don't give him [Huang Can] a way out.

Cao Junwu: Regardless of the minutiae of what exactly happened, even if it was goddamn Guo Li [a former colleague at *Southern Weekly* who now works in another province] who made the changes, the Provincial Propaganda Department is still responsible for it all. They're doing all the directing. Do you think Huang is doing things on his own? Huang is just their personal secretary.

Small clashes continued in the chat group that evening:

Su Yongtong: We don't know what happened January 2. All we know is that all the editors were back in Panyu sleeping, and they received no notice whatsoever. In fact, that is it. That sums it up! Senior managers at our paper received a phone call and went and changed things around. We don't have to worry too much about how exactly the changes happened. If they [the senior managers] want to be made into scapegoats, that's their business!

Jia Jia: Can't we just sort out what happened internally first? Our readers and other people following this online want to know. Don't we want to sort out who exactly was responsible? Aside from Tuo Zhen, someone at the paper must be responsible for this.

Su Yongtong: Now is not the time. Fussing over internal matters will just make things more difficult for us.

Shen Yachuan: I understand, but at least we brothers and sisters outside [the newspaper] should be apprised of the facts. No one wants to look like a fool.

Jia Jia and Shen Yachuan, featured in the dialogue above, are both highly respected journalists in China. During this entire affair, many colleagues from outside the paper felt that the *Southern Weekly* staff simply weren't being forthright enough.

On January 4 and 5, media across China received orders from propaganda authorities to refrain from reporting on the *Southern Weekly* incident. According to leaked internal instructions, internet monitoring authorities had issued a threefold ban: no reporting, no commenting, and no reposting of related materials. Further, anything already posted was to be deleted. Internet controls on this story had been relatively relaxed thus far, but now the hammer was coming down.

Senior propaganda officials clearly regarded this gathering storm at *Southern Weekly* as a challenge to Party leadership. This was something they simply could not tolerate, and they were determined to crush any "rumors" of Tuo Zhen's interference in the editorial process. But in their attempt to stem this growing flood, they never reflected upon the lessons provided all those centuries ago by Yu the Great.

Everyone racking their brains about the nagging question of Tuo Zhen's involvement didn't realize that back on the night of January 2,

Huang Can and provincial propaganda authorities had already iden-
tified a plan of action—a plan that would preemptively grant the propaganda department plausible deniability, even despite the glaringly obvious nature of propaganda officials' involvement.

7

SETTLING ACCOUNTS

An expanded editorial meeting was to be held at the Southern Media Group's offices, including not only the editorial committee but also representatives from various news desks, over which Wang Genghui, Nanfang Media Group's editor, presided. This expanded meeting expanded seemingly endlessly, as many staff members who had not in fact been invited nevertheless wandered in. Attempts were made to wave them away, but to no avail.

Sometime after 7:00 p.m., Huang Can opened the door and peeked inside. Seeing how many people had gathered inside, he immediately stepped back. Perhaps he wasn't psychologically prepared to face so many people. Still more were coming. In order to accommodate staff coming in from outside Guangzhou, the meeting time had already been pushed back to 8:00 p.m.

By the time the meeting started, there were nearly forty people in attendance. Some used their phones to record everything that was said. Fan Chenggang prepared three separate recorders as backup, and he worked with several others in attendance to transcribe the main points of the proceedings in real time, so that most essential points reached the WeChat group within a few seconds of being spoken.

Huang Can and Wu Xiaofeng made presentations in turn, attempting to clarify the events of a few days prior. Nagging questions about Tuo Zhen's role in these events, however, were not clarified, and were arguably made even less clear.

Huang Can shared his version:

As we hadn't gone to print, and the issue was ahead of schedule, we made some changes according to their [the propaganda department's] opinions . . . and we added that short passage that, as everyone has said, included some errors. About that passage, well, of course some of it was drafted by us, and the errors in the draft are entirely ours. We have to take full responsibility for this. . . . I will tell you sincerely that this had nothing to do with Tuo Zhen. But of course, as to whether he saw it, that I really don't know. But for certain, we wrote the text. We wrote the New Year's greeting. Adding those lines, that was based on a recommendation by the propaganda department, but we wrote them ourselves. As for the preface, I'll let Xiaofeng speak on that.

As Zhu Youke, who was present at the meeting, described, Huang Can muttered and mumbled his way through this presentation, turning with each line to look at Wu Xiaofeng, who sat by his side. Huang Can seemed very preoccupied throughout the meeting, and stepped outside at several points without explanation.

When Wu Xiaofeng spoke, he did not address the errors in the passage about Yu the Great taming the floods.

Chief Huang has given us a general summary of what happened. I don't think we'll delve too much into the details today. That might hurt people in the propaganda department. Not chief Tuo, but it might hurt others. I'll just speak about that bit of text on the front page. . . . On January 1, we went to the propaganda office, and they demanded we change the entire thing. . . . A certain comrade at the provincial propaganda office told us, you can't use this image. He gave us two reasons: the first was that Yu the Great was a controversial figure, and second was that the image itself was too dark. We argued about these two points for a long time. . . . We were able to keep the image, but it would have to come with an explanation. . . . As for what this explanation was to say, this all came from a comrade at the propaganda department, saying it should say this and that, from this year to that year, and so on. I took notes on everything they said, and then I arranged it all. . . . As for the text, well, I don't know where things went wrong. I wasn't in a great mood at the time, and there's a problem with my phone's Pinyin input. So, then we ended up with these errors.

Tuo Zhen's anger toward *Southern Weekly* over the so-called rumors of his involvement might be understandable, but provincial propaganda authorities had not exactly been valiant defenders of the truth. From another perspective, given that Tuo Zhen seemingly had not personally written the text, Yang Jibin and others started to worry that "this bucket of shit might be dumped on us editors' heads."

Wang Genghui seemed particularly restless. He stood up and left at 8:30 p.m., heading off to another meeting. He then returned at 10:00 p.m., seeming altogether uninterested in hearing the outcome of the discussion. Cao Junwu and others still wanted to continue talking, but Wang Genghui cut them off, saying it was too late. "We have to let people rest," he said.

Inside the chat group, where journalists were monitoring the discussion, the response was almost instantaneous. "They can't just break it up like that," one member wrote angrily. "Block the doors!" said another. Events inside the room and sentiment outside, where staffers were glued to their smartphone screens, were locked in a kind of tug-of-war. On several occasions senior managers tried to call the meeting to an end and were prevented from doing so by representatives in attendance. The confrontation went on for another hour, until finally it was decided that Chen Mingyang would take the lead in drafting a report of everyone's demands, which would be delivered to senior figures at the paper the next day.

As the meeting ended, Huang Can suddenly discovered that someone from *Southern Weekly*'s television production unit had been videotaping the event. He demanded that the footage be deleted immediately. The journalists, however, were thankfully able to recover the deleted video file as soon as they returned to their desks.

That evening, clouds gathered in the sky, covering the moon and stars, while the air grew damp and cold. After the meeting ended, colleagues went together to the nearby Jinhe Restaurant for a late dinner. Jinhe was a Cantonese-style restaurant with patio seating that was often open into the wee hours of the morning.

More than ten staffers walked over to the restaurant and crowded around a table, pulling over a few extra chairs. When the waitress explained that one pot of soup would make for just nine small bowls, everyone agreed on ordering a second. Although the atmosphere in the meeting had been tense and heated, everyone was still quite relaxed around the dinner table.

Then, just as the soup arrived, Wu Wei received a text message followed by two urgent phone calls. He held the log-in details for the paper's official Weibo account and was being urged to post a statement written by Huang Can that attributed the controversial edits directly to the editorial office. It read:

> The New Year's greeting published in our January 3 special edition was written by this paper's editors according to the theme of "chasing dreams." Rumors circulating on the internet about this greeting are untrue. Due to time pressures and negligence, there are errors in the text. For this, we sincerely apologize to our readers. Our paper did not release the statement that appeared online recently, attributed to our editorial department. We hereby wish to clarify the matter and express our heartfelt thanks to all readers and friends who have supported *Southern Weekly* over the years.

Wu Wei pulled Wu Xiaofeng outside to talk about the pressures he was facing. He urged him to stay strong and not to send out the message, no matter what. He even promised Wu Wei that if his resistance cost him his job, he would write him a strong recommendation for the *21st Century Economic Herald*, another paper under the Southern Media Group umbrella.

Wu Wei reassured Wu Xiaofeng that he would hold out until the end, even if he didn't know where that would lead.

The relentless pressure from Huang that evening drove Wu Wei to "inadvertently" allow his colleagues to see the text. Upon returning to the table, Wu exaggeratedly shouted, "Oh no! I received this text message and carelessly put it where all of you could see. What shall I do now?" He placed his phone on the table, and it was quickly passed around.

Except for Huang Can, virtually every member of the editorial board was at the restaurant that night. Many had taken an ambivalent approach to the flood that had built over the previous few days. But now, Huang Can's actions amounted to selling out the paper's reputation and thus its future. Seeing this text message, everyone was united.

The very thought of releasing Huang's statement through the official *Southern Weekly* account was humiliating. Around the table that night, someone compared it to "not just dumping a pot of shit on our heads but forcing us to eat it."

"That statement must not be sent out. It absolutely must not be sent out," said Wu Xiaofeng.

One of the paper's journalists from Shanghai who joined this dinner remembered it was like watching a group of people all sailing in their own individual directions suddenly climb into a single boat.

Everyone ate their food without relish that evening and hurried back to the editorial office to discuss counterstrategies, leaving behind the rest of the now cold soup.

Soon thereafter, in the early morning of January 6, nearly everyone who had been present around the table sent their own text messages to Huang Can deploring the statement. The five editors responsible for the New Year's edition, meanwhile, sent a joint text message voicing their determined disagreement.

> Chief Can, we have learned that our paper is to release a statement that reads as follows: "The New Year's greeting published in our January 3 special edition was written by this paper's editors according to the theme of 'chasing dreams.' Rumors circulating on the internet about this greeting are untrue. Due to time pressures and negligence, there are errors in the text. For this, we sincerely apologize to our readers. Our paper did not release the statement that appeared online recently, attributed to our editorial department. We hereby wish to clarify the matter and express our heartfelt thanks to all readers and friends who have supported *Southern Weekly* over the years."
>
> We are the editors of the issue mentioned in this statement, and we certainly did not write the text in question. Moreover, exactly how this was written and published was already settled clearly at tonight's meeting. Under these circumstances, if a statement of this kind, so full of erroneous information, is released, we will be left with no other choice but to make the truth of this matter public. We also reserve the right to take further actions.
> Signed,
> Shi Zhe, Cao Junwu, Yang Jibin, Su Yongtong, Ye Weimin

Each sent this note to Huang Can via text message, but no one received a response.

Emotions were also surging in the online chat group, where everyone had heard the news. A growing number of staffers were already suggesting that they scrap the fantasy of negotiations and move directly to a strike or some other more robust action.

Qin Xuan said, "We should go ahead and strike. We should have started already. Otherwise we have no basis for negotiations."

Cao Junwu once again stressed the importance of the *Southern Weekly* brand: "Everything is on the table, but we have to be particularly careful about how we choose to proceed at critical moments. I'll tell you 100 percent sincerely that the *Southern Weekly* brand is not Huang Can's. It doesn't matter to him if it's destroyed. But we love this brand and have a sense of duty. Burning it all down has to be our last resort."

On January 6, newspapers across the country published a story from the official Xinhua News Agency announcing that China was facing its coldest winter in twenty-eight years. Almost immediately, a new online meme took shape based upon this story, using the phrase "Southern weather" as a metaphor for the *Southern Weekly* incident: cold winds had swept away Guangdong's warm sun.

That afternoon, a few members of the editorial board were called to the conference room for a "team meeting." The biggest concern on the minds of their superiors was ensuring that the next issue be published on schedule. The biggest concern for *Southern Weekly* editors, by contrast, was ensuring that Huang's statement not be released on the official Weibo account. Wu Xiaofeng and Zhang Dongming proposed a plan to mitigate tensions: a meeting between representatives from the newspaper and Tuo Zhen at the four-star Zhudao Guesthouse. Chen Mingyang's alternative plan, however, drew more support: a political performance that gave both sides some leeway. Tuo Zhen, in this performance, would make an official inspection tour of the Southern Media Group. While conveying the "spirit" of the recent National Conference of Propaganda Ministers in Beijing to his counterparts in the Guangzhou media, he would at the same time promise to improve management at *Southern Weekly*. Chen Mingyang even imagined a scenario whereby Tuo would make a lighthearted joke, saying: "There are rumors on the internet that I wrote the New Year's greeting, so I've come to collect my freelance fee." Chen's concern was that the more everyone got twisted up in these matters of what exactly had happened, the more complex everything would become. And thus, it was better, he felt, to use a more lighthearted approach to break through these tensions. Unfortunately, the Provincial Propaganda Department never even responded to his proposal.

On the evening of January 6, Chen Mingyang posted an update to the WeChat group:

1. At the meeting this afternoon [attended by members of the editorial board], the discussion centered on the paper's official Weibo account. The basic message from Huang Can and Wang Genghui was that we need to act in accordance with the decisions coming from the Party committee. Everyone, however, voiced their opposition very clearly. For now, the question of posting this statement on the official Weibo account has been shelved. There are, however, still plans to work around this official Weibo account to place the blame on us.
2. Our director went over yesterday to meet with provincial propaganda officials and received assurances that, first, there would be no retributive actions, and second, they would improve news management.
3. Wang Genghui and Huang Can are really focused on delivering the next issue. They have been instructed not only that the issue must come out on schedule, but also that it must meet the *Southern Weekly* standard. . . .
4. We believe that some of us should begin preparing materials, although we won't necessarily use these now. This includes a response to the *Lianhe Zaobao* report, which we won't release immediately. We need to consolidate what we have. As for the plan for the official Weibo account, we'll have to see whether they accept it, and then take things from there.

As before, there were clear divisions among colleagues, who had settled into two distinct and mutually opposed camps. One side advocated a wait-and-see attitude. The other urged everyone not to harbor any illusions and to stay on the offensive.

A little after 5:00 p.m., in a fast-food restaurant near the *Southern Weekly* offices, Mao Zhe, *Southern Weekly*'s general manager in charge of business, circulation, new media, and other areas, worked through a hot bowl of noodles while sharing his pressing moral dilemma with Wu

Chuanzhen. He had just gotten started when yet another call came in from the editor in chief, Huang Can. Mao Zhe set down his bowl and chopsticks and rushed off immediately to Huang's office.

Huang Can intended to make a power play for the password to the paper's official Weibo in the name of the media group's Party committee. Soon, Wu Wei received a call from Mao Zhe, who was sitting in Huang Can's office, relaying a stern demand from Huang. Mao's tone was awkward, but at the same time determined.

By this time, Wu Wei was at his wits' end. Since January 2, Huang Can had repeatedly asked him to post various messages on the official Weibo account assuming "official" responsibility for the incident. So far, he and Mao Zhe had successfully resisted, convincing Huang Can instead to register a separate account called "No Regrets at *Southern Weekly*." But by this point, the battle to preserve the reputation of *Southern Weekly* in the face of Huang's planned statement had gone on for ninety hours.

This was probably the most difficult decision of Wu Wei's life. He had joined *Southern Weekly* in its heyday and become a member of the editorial desk. He couldn't just roll over and accept the newspaper destroying itself like this. Born and raised in Chongqing, an avid sports fan who for many years had worn a baseball cap with his ponytail jutting out the back, Wu was known for his jovial personality. He had never encountered this kind of trouble before. Of course, Wu understood that sooner or later he would have to give up his resistance. "In terms of ownership, I guess they do have a right to ask for it," he said of the log-in details to the official Weibo account. "After all, this isn't my personal property. I have no real justification for keeping it to myself. But I really don't want that statement to come out. First, it destroys the *Southern Weekly*'s reputation; second, it will only make matters worse. I feel a sense of responsibility."

Wu Wei expressed all the objections he had laid out so many times before and warned that he would make his own public statement as soon as he relinquished the password. He could tell the phone was on speaker, and Huang Can interjected: "I can understand you doing that." Wu Wei again stressed that this decision would be judged by history. "Well, that's something I'll have to face," Huang Can responded.

Over the next couple of hours, Wu Wei received nearly thirty phone calls. Seven of these calls were from Huang Can and Mao Zhe, who continued to apply pressure. The other calls, by contrast, were from colleagues, urging him to delay as much as possible. "It was literally like I was being split in two," Wu Wei recalls. As the pressure continued to build, Wu Wei asked Mao Zhe for more time. "I'll send you the password after I've finished writing my personal statement," he said.

It only took Wu a few minutes to write his personal statement. But first he made an urgent call to Jiang Yiping, a veteran editor and senior Southern Media Group executive who had earned the unanimous respect of journalists at *Southern Weekly*. Wu wanted to confirm whether this decision actually came from the group's Party committee, and if so, whether Jiang Yiping could help persuade others in senior management that this was a foolish course.

Ultimately, it turned out that the decision came from the "big three"—Tuo Zhen, Huang Can, and Yang Jian—and not from the Party committee. Someone, most likely either Yang Jian or Huang Can, had passed along a phony Party committee decree.

Jiang Yiping asked Wu whether it would be possible to continue stalling. Wu explained that he had already held out for days, and that Mao Zhe had just called him three times in a row to pressure him yet again.

Jiang immediately called Yang Xingfeng, who already knew there was no hope of resisting. He told Jiang that there was a newly revised draft of the statement, and that this new draft shouldn't create too big a backlash. In reality, however, this revised statement continued to completely deny the provincial propaganda office's involvement in the special issue. Such lies could never be accepted by *Southern Weekly* staff.

Propaganda officials hoped the rest of the world would believe their version of the story—that a bunch of respected reporters had set out to smear the reputations of irreproachable Party cadres.

Wu Wei, finally at the end of his rope after answering another call from Mao Zhe, had just one final question: To whom should I give the password? "Just give it to me," responded Mao.

On the afternoon of January 15 that year, I met with Mao Zhe. Others were milling around the office, so he pointed us to a gray leather sofa at the end of the hallway. He didn't even ask what it was that I wanted, instead just forcing a smile and acknowledging that he had "entered the spotlight."

How had this happened? Just ten days earlier, on January 5, Mao Zhe had been on vacation in southwestern Yunnan province. He had been surprised to receive a phone call from Huang Can demanding that he immediately return to Guangzhou to handle the official Weibo account. He spent that entire night on the phone: talking on the one hand with Huang Can and senior management from the Nanfang Daily Group, and on the other hand with his wife, assessing the situation and the balance of power inside the paper. That night, one call after another, Mao Zhe found himself unable to decide what to do.

"I knew that there was no way out for me. Of course, I knew what sending this statement out meant. . . . But you have to bear the responsibility that comes with your position. If I was an ordinary editor, I could just hide from the situation, saying I was sick in Yunnan, or I could shove it on to Wu Wei. . . . But that's not how I handle things. . . . If we're talking about matters in the abstract, it might seem like I could just stay back and not get involved. But when we're talking about real life and real issues, there's no way I could not get involved. It was a true moral dilemma I was facing," he recalled, shifting uneasily on the leather sofa.

Mao Zhe purchased a plane ticket to Guangzhou for January 6. But then at Huang Can's urging, he shifted his itinerary forward so he could arrive six hours earlier than planned. Huang Can had at one point said that maybe he could just get the password from Wu Wei himself. "I'm not sure why he said that—was he trying to be polite, or what," Mao Zhe said with a bit of effort. "I sort of felt sorry for Huang Can. No one was going to help him."

Mao Zhe had worked at *Southern Weekly* for over a decade, and he had served as the deputy editor in chief in charge of several core fields, including economics. He had a reputation among his colleagues for being even-tempered and honest. When Huang Can's statement was finally posted on the official Weibo account, colleagues were shocked. Chen Mingyang phoned Mao Zhe to say he couldn't understand his decision. "There was just no other way, no other way," Mao Zhe said as his voice faded.

Sitting on the leather sofa, Mao Zhe took on a dignified air for a moment. "That statement was basically true, although it of course also excluded a whole other set of truths," he said. "Some of the things being shared online actually did have factual issues. I can't set the truth aside, and not get the facts straight, just because I want to find a way to relax restraints on our reporting." As for the choices he had made in this situation, he showed no signs of wanting to hide behind any excuses. He just commented, earnestly, "People tend to believe the choices they made are the right ones and will do anything that they can to rationalize them."

As for the juicier details of exactly how things went down, Mao Zhe confessed that he was keeping that to himself. "[There are some details] I can tell you when the time is right. I'll never forget them. I'm not sure I'll ever face such an excruciatingly difficult decision again in my life-time."

At almost the exact moment that he sent the account's password to Mao Zhe via text message, Wu Wei posted a statement on his own Weibo account. According to Sina, the post was made at exactly 9:18 p.m.

> @Fengduan [Wu Wei's online ID]. A statement: I have handed over the @SouthernWeekly account's password to General Manager Mao Zhe, who is now in charge of *Southern Weekly*'s new media. I take no responsibility for the announcement that this account is about to post, or for any other content that it will post in the future. Thank you for your understanding. Wu Wei.

Then, at forty-two seconds after 9:20 p.m., the official *Southern Weekly* Weibo account posted the following:

> To our readers: The New Year's greeting published in our January 3 New Year's special edition was written by this paper's editors accord-ing to the theme of "chasing dreams." All content on the cover of the special issue was also drafted by contributors to our paper. Rumors circulating online are not true. Because we were pressed for time, there were some mistakes in the text, and we apologize to our read-ers for this.

Although officials in the provincial propaganda authorities were not proficient in Weibo, they received prompt notification of this official denial of "the rumors." They probably even felt a sense of relief for a moment, confident that there would be a shift in public opinion. In their minds, who, after all, would doubt a statement from the paper's official account?

Wu Wei knew that *Southern Weekly* needed to respond to the mistaken rumors that were circulating. But Wu also felt that the way they went about it was a mistake. "This official statement could be considered 'true.' But there is an important distinction between something being 'true' and being 'the truth.' Even if every piece of information in that statement was technically correct, it certainly did not represent the whole truth of the matter."

Many found themselves unable to comprehend the hard-line official response that this announcement represented. Among them was veteran journalist Fan Yijin, who said, "This all started off as an internal struggle, involving just a few people. But when they attempted to use the official account to intervene and ruin the paper's reputation, that is when this became a mass movement. *Southern Weekly*'s demands were reasonable and did not pose any direct challenge to the Party's media management system. They should have just given them space to do what they do."

Wu Wei's post was public for nearly half an hour and was shared more than twenty thousand times. But then, Sina Weibo monitors blocked the post from being shared any further. The official *Southern Weekly* statement was shared more than 1.3 million times but featured less than thirty approved comments. Almost any comment, even a lone question mark, would produce that familiar Weibo system prompt: "Your content violates relevant regulations and policies."

The stunning stretch of the Pearl River adjacent to *Southern Weekly* offices is surrounded on both sides by dazzling skyscrapers. And these skyscrapers are illuminated at night by bizarrely over-the-top lighting that makes them appear almost as an illusion. One can easily get lost in these buildings' reflections, floating gently upon the surface of the river. Having just sent out his personal statement on Weibo, Wu Wei sat in one of these apartments, with feelings of frustration gathering and gradually enveloping him. He put his cell phone and computer aside, feeling not the least interest in the storm brewing online. It had been quite a few days since he had put his son to bed. His son was the only person in the world with whom he really wanted to talk tonight. He liked to read Greek myths to him in the peaceful quiet of the night: Apollo and Theseus were distant figures, distant enough that they had nothing to do with *Southern Weekly*.

8

STRUGGLING AMID THE SURGING WATERS

With Huang Can in control of *Southern Weekly*'s official Weibo account, the gravity of the situation became apparent. No longer feeling safe in their offices, staffers secretly decided to relocate to the nearby Golden Bridge Hotel. Yang Jibin called it the editorial office in exile.

The Golden Bridge Hotel is a low-key four-star hotel just two hundred meters from the Southern Media Group headquarters. A crowd of teary, red-eyed editors and reporters sat on the floor in two deluxe suites. They could not get over the surrender of the paper's official Weibo account, which had occurred just an hour earlier. It's easy to understand their sense of despair: *Southern Weekly*, it seemed, was finished.

Not long after the official Weibo account had been commandeered, Yang Jian called a meeting with staffers in the conference room, but they refused. At 9:26 p.m. that night, as several editors were waiting at the elevators, preparing to leave the office, Huang Can and Mao Zhe suddenly appeared and reminded them of the meeting. A young female editor responded coldly: "What use is there in explaining now?" She turned to the stiff-faced editor in chief: "You will be remembered by history as a criminal, a willing executioner."

That was a night of sadness, despair, shock, confusion, and even excitement. All types of emotions that don't usually cross paths suddenly came together. Many of the younger contributors to *Southern Weekly* are of the one-child generation, who grew up in the relatively calm and stable environment of China's reform era. They were not accustomed to the type of viciousness emerging in this incident; even as kids, when they got into arguments with friends, these arguments never spiraled into the type of full-on violence with which the older generation raised in the Cultural Revolution was all too familiar. The panic of January 6, as a result, left them with an impending feeling that the end was near.

Qin Xuan's dread continued to grow that night. As the crisis continued to expand, Qin began to have all types of mixed feelings. He would feel terrified. But then he would also think that he had to finish what he had started. But then he would comfort himself by thinking, "If we don't make it into a big deal, it won't be a big deal." He worried about going to prison, but he eventually heard from Shi Zhe that Hu Chunhua had guaranteed that no one was going to prison. "I immediately hugged him and relaxed a little. I felt quite powerless."

The moment that Cao Junwu opened the door to the hotel suite and saw his colleagues, his emotions overpowered him, and he could not refrain from sobbing uncontrollably, like a frightened child. As the tears streamed down his face, the heroic appearance that he took on in Age of Empires disappeared in a flash.

"What's the use in crying? Get writing!" Deng Ke yelled. Sounding a bit like a supervisor ordering his subordinate around, Deng's command unexpectedly shattered the otherwise bleak mood that night.

After the official statement had been posted, rage spread through the WeChat group: "Shit, shit, shit!" "Fuck!" "I feel cold all over," "I'm crying," "Our enemies are too cruel," "Mother—," "Strike," "No hesitation," "Set aside all illusions, set them aside completely."

Shi Zhe, who never said a word in the paper's WeChat group, suddenly added a comment: "Don't get overwhelmed. No one can give up now. If anyone does give in, I'll never forgive you."

Southern Weekly's unique culture became most apparent in these "last of days." On an average day, everyone would do their own thing, with nothing really bringing everyone together into a fully cohesive team. But at this moment when the paper's core values were in danger, a powerful sense of cohesion suddenly emerged. What was under threat was no longer just a workplace. It was a family.

That night, many former staffers for *Southern Weekly* were also shedding tears. Many of them had a deep attachment to this paper, a special connection that one could not find at any other media outlet. It was almost like a type of faith, an unbreakable bond to a spiritual home. As Zuo Fang, one of the founding editors of *Southern Weekly*, once said, "The majority of *Southern Weekly*'s team joined our paper because they identify with our founding ideals. Any attempt to change these will inevitably create a real conflict." One of the paper's best reporters, Li Haipeng, also wrote about this sense of attachment in one of his interview write-ups: "We can't be young forever, we can't be passionate forever. But we will never forget our vision of a better world."

The dual statements from *Southern Weekly*'s and Wu Wei's Weibo accounts reignited online discussions. Even @People'sDaily, the official account of the Party Central newspaper, could not resist getting involved. Curiously, they posted only a "surprised" emoticon, showing a face with notable drops of sweat and two eyes wide open—the shortest of the *People's Daily* account's more than four thousand posts.

And then, suddenly at midnight that night, everything changed. In Chen Ming's words, someone was sent from above to save *Southern Weekly*. That someone was Zeng Li, a sixty-one-year-old seasoned media professional with a bit of a childish temperament. Zeng was as fond of foul language as he was of laughter, and he typically spent more than ten hours a day absorbed in the online world. He was an internal examiner of the paper's contents, a post that does not typically earn—or indeed deserve—much affection. Most staffers, however, had gradually warmed up to Zeng. That night, he posted a piece under his real name titled "Who Really Changed the *Southern Weekly* New Year's Edition," in which he provided an analysis of the situation as follows:

> Who made the changes to *Southern Weekly*'s New Year cover heading and greetings? We can't say for sure until we hear from the propaganda authorities and the editors, but we can say with certainty that this was not a decision made solely by the editors. The editors had already signed off on their content and agreed that it was ready to be printed. It seems highly unlikely that the same editors would then go and request all types of changes after the fact.

The most significant aspect of this post was not what Zeng Li said, but rather his identity: a core media figure with experience in both official and internal review of media content who had long been trusted by the Party. His post was a rhetorical atom bomb in this growing conflict: it was the encouragement *Southern Weekly* and its supporters so desperately needed at this moment.

Actually, by the time it was discovered, Zeng Li's post had already been sitting on his not-so-lively blog for seven or eight hours. And then, just as the situation at *Southern Weekly* was heating up, the post was suddenly seen, shared, and commented on virally on Weibo. The key moment for Zeng Li was 4:58 p.m. on January 6, when he held his mouse in his right hand and applied slight pressure via his index finger without really giving it too much thought. This turned out to be the most important single click of his life.

Prior to making this decision, Zeng Li spoke on the phone with a senior figure in the Southern Media Group. This senior figure agreed on the necessity of revealing the propaganda authorities' crude handling of this matter, voicing his confidence that going public was in the group's interest. Yet this senior figure also admitted that there was little he could do other than quietly voice his support.

Among the many people working at *Southern Weekly*, Zeng Li stood out for his lack of scholarly airs. He did not specialize in refined formulations, preferring instead to frequently resort to foul language and dirty jokes. As a young man he had worked in agriculture and stoked the furnace in a metal refinery. These experiences had endowed him with the type of directness and fortitude often found among those who work the most exhausting of jobs just to put food on the table. But Zeng Li also had his "obedient" side: from a young age, he had served as a cog in the Chinese Communist Party's propaganda machinery. Even during his tenure at *Southern Weekly*, he appeared to be a reliably obedient devotee of the Party's media regulations.

In the early 1960s, in an elementary school classroom in Zhanjiang, Guangdong, a young man seeking praise from his teachers instead received an unforgettable blow to his confidence. He handed in an essay in response to the prompt "Describe a time when you helped others." His response: "On a dark and chilly morning, I went to a store two hours before it opened to buy fish. Unfortunately, there were not enough fish for everyone waiting in line, and I just happened to get the last one. A few people in line were complaining, and there was an elderly lady behind me who was left with no fish. So I gave her my lucky fish." His teacher's response: "How, in a socialist country, could there not be enough fish for everyone? This story smears our great socialist system." His teacher had long before mastered the art of singing vapid songs of praise in an era of tragedy and took it as her mission to teach her students to do the same.

That young man was Zeng Li. His teacher's unforgiving comments were undoubtedly tied to his class background. You see, in the early years of the People's Republic, he had made the mistake of being born to a member of the "five black elements." In the discursive system that Mao forced upon China, the "five black elements" were enemies of the ruling proletariat, and the son of a class enemy was destined to also be a class enemy. From a young age, Zeng Li was forced to repeatedly watch "the masses" struggle against his own father. As a result, as he grew older he instinctively yearned for approval from the Party, doing everything in his power to prove that he was different.

From his classroom experience as a child, Zeng Li learned how to tell the type of lies the Party required. From the barren countryside to a smoky metal refinery plant, Zeng Li became a grassroots Party propagandist, a role that eventually defined his career. Propaganda is a tool that the Party uses both to control the people and to direct internal struggles; Zeng Li's job in the refinery was to keep the propaganda coming at all times.

"First you criticize this, then you criticize that. We are criticizing Lin Biao, Confucius, and Deng Xiaoping, and then the next thing you know we are criticizing the Gang of Four. Then we are suddenly singling out particular people in the plant for criticism. This is just what those of us who did propaganda full-time had to do," he reflected in his choppy Cantonese-style Mandarin. He refused to shy away from the darker side of his work, adding, "In 1980, I saw that the factory boss was growing more powerful. So I followed along with the shifting winds, and gradually kept my distance from the party secretary. That was just what you did. It worked."

While working in the countryside, Zeng Li fell in love for the first time. And even after he left the countryside, he and his ex-girlfriend kept in touch and remained friends. Zeng Li was even open about all of this with his wife: such frankness about earlier romantic relationships was rare among people of Zeng's generation in China.

In his daily life, Zeng Li always maintained a straightforward character. But perhaps due to that one assignment in his childhood, he tended to hide his true opinions. This tendency led him to feel an extreme sense of shock when he first started as an internal reviewer at *Southern Weekly*. He thought to himself, slightly puzzled, these writers actually want to share their real thoughts in public? Are they crazy?

In the history of the People's Republic, the 1980s were a period of unrivaled openness. Western values and images of the West's dazzling lifestyles came flooding into China. Zeng Li, who already had his doubts about the Party and its ideals, began to have a sense that there was a freer and indeed better world beyond China's borders. Recognizing the risk of such thinking, the authorities called for mass critiques of "bourgeois liberalization" in the mid-1980s. Zeng Li was left to organize these criticism sessions, while at the same time knowing deep down that what everyone was criticizing was right, and what everyone was promoting was in fact wrong.

In 2008, Zeng Li was appointed as a special assistant to the editors of *Southern Weekly*. In reality, he was a full-time internal examiner who had been sent by the Southern Media Group to watch over the rabble-rousing *Southern Weekly*. Before long, Zeng was also named deputy head of the provincial propaganda authorities' news commentary group, an important link in the censorship system, with the power to determine which published reports had "political problems."

Zeng Li was in Shenzhen when he heard about *Lianhe Zaobao*'s supposed "refutation of rumors." He felt a rage building up that he simply could not suppress. Two weeks later, recounting that moment in his office, he still could not hold himself back from forcefully smacking the dark brown coffee table a few times: "This is wrong! Dammit, how could this be OK?" Zeng Li could see very clearly that the propaganda officials' claims that they "had nothing to do with this" put *Southern Weekly* in a very tricky situation.

Like many other *Southern Weekly* staff, Zeng Li's anger had been building long before this controversy.

In his son Zeng Rong's eyes, Zeng Li was quite the trailblazing senior citizen. A few years earlier, he had begun to explore the internet, and before he knew it, he had become lost on the information super-highway. "Every day, besides the time he spent eating and sleeping, he was on the web." He soon abandoned all his other hobbies: photography, sports, and many others.

In Zeng Li's eyes, the internet was simply amazing. In the past, he only had a broad conception of the evils of dictatorship, the issue of inequality, and the tragic lives of the underclass. But the internet placed these shocking realities directly before his eyes. "Shit, I mean, shit," he would often mutter while reading the news.

While he still worked within the system, Zeng Li only read. But in 2011, on the day that he retired his official position, he rediscovered his voice after all those decades. He registered an online ID under the name of "Clear-headed sixty-year-old" and became active online. He engaged in spirited debates with conservatives and let off some of his anger by "cursing the Cultural Revolution, cursing Mao, cursing all of those inhuman things we have faced in this life."

Trouble came knocking on his door quickly, however. Sometimes internet censors would delete posts that he thought were not in the least politically sensitive. Zeng Li couldn't decide whether he should laugh or cry at the fact that he was still officially an internal examiner at one of China's best-known weeklies, and that his main responsibility in this position was to identify politically risky content. If even he couldn't figure out what posts might be sensitive, what luck was anyone else going to have? These online experiences helped him better understand the situations regularly faced by his colleagues at *Southern Weekly* and led him to be a bit more reserved in the use of his own red pen.

The Southern Media Group had set up an internal examination system precisely to lower political risk and thereby maximize profits. But editors and journalists at the paper tended to characterize this internal examination system as a self-castration. Accordingly, many contributors held people like Zeng Li and their red pens in disdain. Every week when it came time to prepare a new issue, *Southern Weekly*'s editors would file in and out of his office, lobbying against his concerns about all types of supposedly sensitive topics.

There were two completely different Zeng Lis: one in the internal examination office and another in the online world. He once explained this situation as follows:

> There's a divider in my brain. The left side of my brain is used for examining reports in accordance with political requirements. The right side of my brain embraces free expression on the internet. I can't confuse the two. I must keep them separate, or else I'd be in big trouble. I wouldn't go so far as to say that this is a symptom of multiple personality disorder. Rather, to put a positive spin on it, maybe it's a sign of multilayered thinking.

Zeng Li was once asked how he felt, as an external examiner, about the frequent deletion of his own online commentaries. He began by responding, "Well, that's different." But then he paused for a moment before admitting, "I could say it's different, but actually it's not. I feel like the things that I have written that are deleted are 100 percent true. But at the same time, these essays that are cut from the paper, they are also 100 percent true."

After experiencing such internal debates countless times, Zeng Li began to really understand the sense of commitment that *Southern Weekly* journalists felt toward their reporting. For them, their work was more than just something they did for a salary. It was also part of a process of building a more equal and free China.

Zeng Li had grown from the young man passing his fish to the woman behind him into the thoughtful man in the office's makeshift internal examiner room; his conscience had never changed. Once he really got to know *Southern Weekly*, Zeng Li admired the dedication of the paper's editors and journalists.

In 2009, *Southern Weekly* was preparing a shocking report on government officials hiring people to set up "black jails" [translator's note: secret prisons operating beyond the already quite unaccountable legal system] in Beijing to jail, hide, and abuse petitioners. Zeng Li again faced the type of internal struggle that he often faced in his position. He muttered "shit" again as hellish visions of these black jails flashed before his eyes. He felt this story needed to be told. But at the same time, he feared that the report would infuriate the authorities. So, he worked closely with the editors, finding the best way to avoid risks by deleting some sensitive words. In this process, he became far more than an internal examiner: he became a true colleague.

Then, on January 6, 2013, Zeng Li became more than a colleague. He became a hero who stood up to the dictatorial system, earning him a level of respect that eluded all other news examiners. Zeng Li would always respond modestly to others' praise: "All I am doing is just not going against my conscience, that's it. As for anything beyond that, what power do I have to go against this system?"

At the end of his buzzworthy blog post, Zeng Li wrote:

> As a member of the news examination team, it is technically a violation of regulations for me to talk so openly. But this situation is

already boiling over. Dozens of *Southern Weekly* writers and contributors, including myself, have had their Weibo accounts frozen
and are unable to share their stories. In this context, I can no longer
keep silent.

Zeng's post suddenly tore open the iron curtain around the news examination system. We can't forget that, at a Ministry of Foreign Affairs
press conference just a few days earlier, Ministry of Foreign Affairs of
Japan spokesperson Hua Chunying had claimed in response to a Japa-
nese journalist's question about the developments at *Southern Weekly*
that "I want to point out that there's no so-called censorship of media in
China. The Chinese government protects journalists' freedom."

Three months after Zeng Li's post, Deng Ke sighed as he asked his
colleagues, "How did such an open mind grow and blossom in this sixty-
year-old in the most conservative post in our entire organization?" But
by the time Deng asked this question, Zeng Li was no longer able to
answer.

9

THE BANALITY OF EVIL

Near 10:00 p.m. on January 6 in the editorial office in exile, Wu Xiaofeng suddenly shouted, "I say, let's go on strike." And while they were at it, he added, they might as well make everything they knew public. Colleagues had never seen Wu Xiaofeng quite so restless, as if he were on the verge of a breakdown.

Xiao Hua, standing in the middle of the room, read a statement aloud:

> Urgent! After a day of relentless attacks and a spirited defense, we lost control of *Southern Weekly*'s official Weibo account! The announcement posted from this account does not represent the opinions of our editorial staff and only came about after the authorities applied unrelenting pressure on our management. The editors at *Southern Weekly* will fight to the end against this deceptive statement. Until this situation is resolved, we will not participate in any further editing at the paper. Please everyone, do all that you can within reason to defend *Southern Weekly*!

This was one version of a statement from the *Southern Weekly* team. Some departments were still anxiously seeking feedback. Wu Chuanzhen was trying his best to hold back the statement's release, hoping that a decision would only be made after all the mid-level managers arrived. But Xiao Hua shouted nervously, "I have already tried to cool them down for ten minutes, but I'm not sure how much longer I can hold them back!"

Shouts came from all directions: "We still haven't posted this?"

Soon two more departments stated that they agreed in principle with the statement, but that they also agreed with the recommendation to delay making it public. Eventually, this decision to delay meant that the statement was never officially released. Facing seemingly endless internal disputes, Ye Biao, Zhang Zhe, and a few other reporters just went ahead and posted the statement on their own Weibo feeds.

Reflecting on the initial days of this affair, what Cao Junwu remembered most vividly was the sheer number of leaks, saying, "There was no planning or strategy. It was just a cycle of irritating stimuli and counterresponses."

At 10:12 that evening, Huang Can called Xiao Hua. Xiao Hua switched to speaker phone, and Deng Ke hurried to record the conversation on his iPhone. Lu Zongru and others stood by listening in. The conversation that followed brought many to tears.

"Hello, Xiao Hua?"

"Hello, Manager Huang."

"I'm sorry, you all are probably . . . everyone's miserable. Everyone is feeling really down, including Mao Zhe, even including myself. But there are some things I need to tell everyone . . . the way you all feel, of course this is not right, but I do need to explain this situation about the Weibo account. Now some of the senior management from our parent company are here, and I hope we can all exchange ideas and communicate. Of course, I understand how everyone feels. I think Mao Zhe is probably taking this the hardest, so I—"

Deng Ke couldn't stop himself from interrupting, "How are you feeling, Manager Huang? Huh?"

"I'm feeling pretty blue."

"*Pretty* blue, huh, General Manager Huang?" Deng Ke responded, emphasizing "pretty."

"I'm really down, just like everyone else."

"Huang, you trashed all the respect that *Southern Weekly* has earned over the past thirty years. We're done, Huang, we're done," Deng Ke said.

After a moment of silence, Deng Ke added, "What kind of chief editor does something like this?"

Chen Mingyang could not resist piling on, "There's really no explanation for doing something like this to your own editorial board."

Deng Ke added, "If you aren't driven by personal interest, then why don't you just quit in protest?"

"I—ah—"

"Tell us. We're listening, tell us," Deng Ke responded.

"We are all listening. And we are recording this conversation. How will history view this decision?" Chen Mingyang asked, enunciating each word carefully.

"So, as I said, I need to explain—"

"General Manager Huang, no matter how long you live—another thirty, even another fifty years, I'll never forget this," Deng Ke interjected.

"I'm also very conflicted. Of course, I know that everyone is really unhappy with what I have done, but I just could not think of any better way to handle this. We have discussed back and forth so many times how to respond to some questions raised by the public," Huang Can said.

"General Manager Huang, what were you doing this afternoon?" Chen Mingyang asked pointedly.

"This afternoon we also discussed this issue, but we really didn't . . . we felt like this may be the only option that we could think of, although there may be better approaches . . . although this wasn't the best option, it was really the only option, because we couldn't just not reply—"

"General Manager Huang, there is no way that we could ever accept this," Huang Xiao responded, trying his best to control his emotions. "Right now, we are all very emotional, maybe we should cool down and talk later."

Everyone involved in this angry exchange with Huang Can, accusing him of selling out the paper's core values, should have already known that these core values were not his priority.

In the Southern Media Group, the head of the paper's Party committee is a senior managerial position. In 2009, Huang Can, originally the managing editor of the *Nanfang Daily*'s major news department, was promoted to this position and named the editor in chief of *Southern Weekly*.

Like previous managers, Huang Can took a proactive approach to working with his colleagues after arriving at his new position. Huang had worked night shifts for more than a decade at *Nanfang Daily*, but because he was a deputy to one of the two senior managerial cadres in the department, he was constrained by a lack of real power. Once he landed a position where he could make a name for himself, Huang became extremely smug as he bade farewell to his former colleagues.

Huang Can was intoxicated by power. And this power just happened to arrive in his hands at a moment when the entire Southern Media Group was becoming increasingly "official." A number of contributors with real backbone and reporting skills had been silenced, one after another.

Now that Huang could finally wield power on his own, he was eager to establish his authority. But at *Southern Weekly*, where equality and strong personalities coexisted and freedom was the guiding principle, Huang Can's aspirational authority was doomed to face strong resistance and even made him the butt of jokes.

For example, once at a weekly meeting, someone referred to the writing style used in the *New Yorker*. Huang Can immediately asked, "What is the *New Yorker*?" Everyone was shocked. At the next weekly meeting, Huang Can commented, "I looked it up; the *New Yorker* is an American magazine." His frankness yet again shocked everyone in the room.

The new editor in chief's use of vulgar language also left a deep impression upon his colleagues. In a play on words, Huang Can once told reporters that they "can piss the farthest if they put themselves on a high pedestal." His critical comments on proposed drafts were also painfully blunt. In one case, he simply wrote, "Unintelligible bullshit."

Huang Can came from a scholarly family. His father was a researcher in a distinguished library, and Huang himself had received extensive training in calligraphy. This much could be seen in every newspaper layout that his red pen ever touched, which would be changed forever in more ways than one. Tragically, Huang had few opportunities in his post at *Southern Weekly* to show his more refined side.

When Huang Can found himself sitting on the edge of an erupting volcano at the start of 2013, he was no longer the self-assured man who first took on his position. In order to please his superiors, he not only strictly enforced any orders from propaganda department officials, but also went far beyond these orders to ensure that the paper steered well clear of any potentially sensitive topics. When the thirty-two pages of each issue's layout were placed in front of him, his eyes would cautiously scan every page, as if each character had a potential landmine hiding beneath it. Cao Junwu described Huang as a perverse emperor who did whatever he could to satisfy those above him while reigning with an iron fist over those below him. It wasn't even concern about trouble at *Southern Weekly* messing up his future career prospects that kept him up at night; rather, it seemed that even the thought of making his superiors unhappy in any way left Huang Can feeling extremely uneasy.

Caution generates more caution. Fear generates more fear. At some point, Huang Can underwent a real change, which Chen Mingyang described as "fully internalizing the Party line." This change heightened his sensitivity to nearly comic proportions.

While preparing a special issue on the Eighteenth Party Congress, photo editors chose a picture of a child standing in front of a school in rural China. Just behind the child, you could see the characters for "the people" (*renmin*) written on the wall: such state slogans are such common decorations on school walls that most passersby would not even notice. Yet to everyone's surprise, Huang Can notified the photo editors that they couldn't use this picture, "because it is not clear what you intend to say with these two characters for 'the people.'"

Zhu Youke, editor of the culture section, shared memories of many other curious encounters with Huang Can. One of the articles that he wrote was about a poet who had once joined the Communist Party of India but later decided to leave the party. Huang Can felt that it was not ideal to mention someone quitting a Communist Party, so Zhu Youke changed the wording to simply refer to the poet as a "former Communist Party member." Huang Can agreed to this change but still seemed slightly troubled by the reference. Only later when the story was published did Zhu Youke notice that the poet was referred to simply as "a member of the Communist Party of India."

In an investigative article looking into Chinese students applying to the top American universities, one section of the report referred to the involvement of a "Communist Youth League Branch Secretary." Puzzlingly, Huang Can changed this reference to "class monitor."

For a considerable period after Huang Can joined *Southern Weekly*, the paper managed to avoid criticisms from the news commentary group that examined and critiqued media publications after the fact. Like a surfboard tied to a pole, the paper experienced a moment of tumultuous stability. Huang Can proudly declared that not everyone could manage the paper this well, reminding his colleagues that they all would have been "destroyed" many times over were it not for his assistance.

Another source of Huang Can's self-flattery was his method of "testing the winds." After the Wenzhou high-speed train accident occurred in 2011, Huang first only allowed us to publish one small image with two brief lines referring to the accident. This was a way of testing the propaganda department's stance. When he discovered that this did not provoke the authorities' anger, he permitted a little more reporting on the accident in the next issue. Then he allowed some more in the subsequent issue. It may have made sense to him, but for a media outlet, where speed is everything, Huang's "testing the winds" approach was a massive joke, leaving the paper flapping in censorial winds even as the news cycle moved onward.

Su Yongtong recounted that Huang Can particularly enjoyed changing headlines. However, at times, he would inadvertently make headlines even more provocative than they were originally. "I remember one time I did a report on coal mines and for some reason he changed the title to 'A Darkness Even Darker than Coal.' I thought, sure, if you think the other censors will be ok with that." Su felt that it may be unfair to claim that Huang Can did not care about *Southern Weekly*. Rather, he actually may not have fully understood what he was doing. "He compromised far too much, had no clear values or stance, and generally speaking his thinking was utterly illogical."

Cao Junwu expressed the same sentiment far more directly: "The biggest problem with Huang Can is not that he's a bad guy. The problem is that he's an idiot."

Huang Can's office was right below the *Southern Weekly* editor's office. Although the two offices were only a floor apart, they felt like two completely different worlds, gradually drifting ever further apart. Conflict between the editor in chief and the news team was growing by the day on such core issues as the paper's purpose and which audience it was to target: the general public or the censors. Huang Can, who did not deal well with confrontation, began to act in an increasingly confrontational manner.

At home, Huang Can had a beautiful wife who worked in banking and a son who was just entering adolescence. Friends of the family saw that Huang Can's authority at home was not built on brute force. Colleagues remembered some heartwarming scenes from trips with the

THE BANALITY OF EVIL

family: Huang chatting casually with his son on a bike ride or picking reeds or skipping stones on riverbanks on the edge of the city. Stories like this led people to ask, are we talking about the same Huang Can?

Huang Can was a sturdy guy. His hair was short, and his face was square. He liked to play any sports involving nets: badminton or tennis. Although there was no net in his office, the "unruly" editors would knock on his office door and square off with him across his big dark brown desk, engaging in back-and-forth about his endless cuts. Such disrespect to a superior would have been unthinkable at *Nanfang Daily*, where Huang had spent most of his career. But in a real clash of cultures, from the perspective of the editors on the other side of his desk, Huang's arrogance and rudeness were unthinkable at *Southern Weekly*. Cao Junwu described a typical visit to Huang Can's office as follows: "Usually he would be leaning back in his chair, with his head tilted up slightly, his eyes looking down toward you. He would avoid all eye contact and say some completely illogical things. Then you would know there was no fucking way your story was getting published."

"My personality is such that I don't like to explain myself, but I also refuse to compromise." Going head to head with Huang Can left Su Yongtong, who has a naturally shy disposition, exhausted. He recalled, "I'm not good with coming up with some type of excuse to trick my boss, I just can't do it. And I can't really fight too enthusiastically, even for something I believe in. I just prefer a rational discussion. [Convincing Huang Can] is extremely difficult, even borderline impossible. . . . Sometimes I had to ask for help from Cao Junwu."

Su Yongtong was in awe of another relatively outspoken media outlet in China: *Caijing*. Caixin Media was a professional media group whose managers and contributors were all on the same page, working together against the censorship system. By contrast, at *Southern Weekly*, contributors and editors found themselves forced to square off with the editor in chief. Whenever an issue was about to be published, basically everyone had to hurry to Huang Can's office to attempt to rescue overedited or completely rejected pieces. Su Yongtong remembered that he was only able to save at most two or three out of every ten pieces that faced trouble on Huang Can's desk: "I only had a real feeling of accomplishment when I managed to rescue a few things from being dropped. But this left me with no sense of true journalistic dignity, because anything that I really wanted to write about simply had no chance of making it through this process."

In the past, there had been some "big personalities" at *Southern Weekly* who would express their dissatisfaction with managerial decisions very brazenly, even openly criticizing officials' decisions. But as Ye Weimin remembers, although Huang Can made some of the most indefensible editorial decisions in the history of the paper, open challenges to his authority grew increasingly rare. "We would just try to ignore him," he remembered.

Yang Jibin was staying at Cao Junwu's home in 2010 and remembers being completely shocked at Cao's appearance and spirits after getting off work one day: "Cao is over 1.8 meters tall, but when he came home that day, he looked like he had shrunk to just 1.4 meters." Cao Junwu had just been absolutely berated by Huang Can during an argument over an article: in his words, he had been "scolded like a naughty grandchild." Yang Jibin recounted, "Trying to make sense of our passive response to Huang Can, I think we were all just too new. All of a sudden we are editors at this paper, but to be frank we're not the most experienced people, and we actually don't have that much authority in the grand scheme of things. We also need to factor in the fact that quite a few of us had been promoted to our positions by none other than Huang Can. When it comes down to it, maybe we felt grateful to him, and thus hesitated to oppose him. We were new to all of this. It was only in the second half of 2012 that we began to realize that this was a real problem."

Eventually, Cao Junwu and Huang Can had a massive argument in the production room. According to eyewitnesses, Cao and Huang were almost at one another's throats.

In the eyes of his college classmates and former colleagues, Huang Can had some weaknesses: he wasn't a great student, he wasn't an avid user of the internet, and he didn't keep up with the latest trends. But people who knew him had a hard time wrapping their heads around the extent of his clash with *Southern Weekly*'s values. A former colleague commented that Huang Can's managerial approach at *Southern Weekly* was a product not of his personal values but rather of his desire to be promoted: Huang, in his description, was no hyper-nationalist and even bemoaned in private the Chinese Communist Party's rule and the shortcomings in the system. "He never showed any sort of sympathy for Mao Zedong or any of that."

But some of the encounters that people at *Southern Weekly* were having with Huang Can left them with a completely different impression.

Once, the culture section invited an elderly translator who had worked for Mao Zedong, Zhou Enlai, and Deng Xiaoping to write an article reflecting on his experiences. They intended to use a photograph of this translator together with Deng Xiaoping. But Huang Can asked, "Does he have a photograph with Mao?" After learning that he didn't have such a photo, Huang Can sighed and commented, "If he had a picture with Chairman Mao, that would be great."

Other colleagues were shocked to notice that Huang Can's WeChat profile picture was none other than an image of Stalin. Everyone at *Southern Weekly* had a difficult time making sense of this: for them, Stalin was a totalitarian dictator, not someone to emulate.

"Once while scolding us, he said 'people say you are a traitor paper, that you are slaves to the West, and that you'd happily help the West invade China. If you ask me, I think they're right!'" Chen Mingyang remembered being deeply disappointed by such comments: "Sure, on the values question, we had conflicts with Huang Can. But he should know that we do love our country and culture."

Different people have different impressions of Huang Can, painting a very complex portrait of his character. But all of this seeming complexity may have actually been a product of a fundamental simplicity, even banality. One editor commented that Huang Can's behavior at *Southern Weekly* brought to his mind a concept first developed by Hannah Arendt: the banality of evil.

During World War II, Adolf Eichmann signed the execution orders for tens of thousands of European Jews: there was no denying that he was guilty of crimes against humanity. In 1960, when Eichmann was put on trial in Jerusalem, Hannah Arendt sat in on his trial as a correspondent for the *New Yorker*. What shocked Arendt most in the trial was that this truly evil Nazi seemed to have no clear value judgments about his victims or the war in which he had played such an important role. He simply said that he was "following orders," and he never even put deeper thought into the ways in which the Nazi system fed true evil. He simply wanted to make his way up the ladder of command. And at the end of the day, he did not seem to fully grasp what he had done. Arendt concluded that the type of evil that Eichmann represented was all too common in this world. Anyone had the potential to become numb and obedient, enacting orders from above without further reflection, like an evil automaton.

Deceiving the masses? Hiding the truth? It probably never crossed Huang Can's mind that he was doing these things.

In the figure of Huang Can, *Southern Weekly*'s reporters and editors were able to bear witness to a person who had been integrated into "the system" completely. He was in that sense no different from Tuo Zhen: both displayed high levels of trust in the Party and a desire, based in a genuine sense of loyalty, to defend the Party to the very end. Even within the Party-state system, such genuinely loyal officials are rare.

But just as some colleagues at *Southern Weekly* assumed, such loyalty is rewarded.

10

THE LONGEST NIGHT

Once the management confiscated the paper's Weibo account, a temporary planning group known as "Frontal Command" (short for "Frontal Assault on the Enemy Command Center") was formed by staff to make decisions on major issues. The group was composed mainly of members of the paper's editorial board, with the opinions of Chen Mingyang, who had been at the paper the longest, carrying the most weight. Chen later acknowledged that from this point onward he came to play an increasingly important role in the decision-making process; at the same time, he emphasized that *Southern Weekly* had always cherished equality among staff and that his input had never been binding. "I never abused everyone's trust—regardless of whether such trust actually existed."

Chen was smoking like a chimney throughout this entire ordeal. Although he had already developed a horrible cough, he still couldn't stop himself from smoking another cigarette. When he had something to think over, he would sit thinking and smoking for an entire day, leaving in his wake a few empty packs of Yellow Crane Tower cigarettes.

According to Chen, the "Frontal Command's" decision-making process basically followed Robert's Rules of Order: "a motion, followed by the sharing of opinions, with everyone allowed to speak once. No interruptions. If there are disagreements, then everyone shares their opinions again, before a final vote."

But during later discussions, another group member told me that there was no such robust decision-making process. In reality, the *Southern Weekly* culture remained the same as ever, even in a moment of crisis: equality, consideration, the right to express one's opinions—and as a result, a reliably vibrant but unwieldy atmosphere. The elements that were usually lacking in the *Southern Weekly* decision-making process were then still lacking in this moment of crisis: a standardized workflow, a logical decision-making process, and sufficient power to implement decisions.

An internal investigation of these events was eventually released under the name of the Professional Ethics Committee of Southern Weekly. Although this committee's name may seem old and dusty, many felt that the name actually suited it perfectly, precisely for this reason. First of all, Chen Mingyang was the founder of the committee. And second, the dusty name matched the dusty content of the report perfectly.

Prior to the report's release, Chen Mingyang had discussed the idea of abandoning references to the *Southern Weekly* editorial board or editorial committee. In fact, while the editorial committee should have been meeting regularly to discuss such matters, under the influence of Huang Can the committee had long since gone idle. There were three members of the committee who had only joined within the last year, and as a result simply had no idea how to conduct an editorial committee meeting. It was thus out of a concern for abiding by the proper approval process that any references to these two official bodies within the report were dropped. The "Frontal Command" was so focused upon the process that when they met they even spent time calculating how many ballots the editorial committee would have in a vote, how big a proportion was necessary to pass a motion, and even whether people who were not present, such as Mao Zhe or Wu Zhiquan (an administrative director), qualified as part of the committee.

Overthinking process and deliberating endlessly over minute details—some colleagues viewed these as telltale signs that the paper was run by hardheaded bookworms unsuited to getting anything done.

There were not enough ashtrays, so the cigarette butts piled up like little mountains inside participants' teacups. In those sleepless nights, numerous hands hurriedly crashed down on keyboards, aiming to document the truths of Tuo Zhen's crude management style. The "Frontal

Command" decided unanimously that out of concern for everyone's safety, they would refrain from directly denouncing the entire censorship system: "We affirm that we support the principle of the Party guiding the media." Although this wasn't a completely sincere declaration, this line was nevertheless placed at a prominent location in the eventual statement. Honestly, the authors simply felt that a fight for true freedom of the press in a one-party dictatorship was impossible.

At 10:27 p.m., the joint statement signed by ninety-six contributors was published on Weibo, notifying the general public that the paper's official Weibo account had already been compromised and that the explanation posted there was not accurate. "We will continue to distribute accurate information through open channels." The signatures were collected via phone and WeChat with surprising efficiency.

The lights in the suite were relatively dim. Editorial staff members were spread across the suite's beds and floor. Occasionally their fingers would move across their touch screens, busy either sharing information with the outside world or closely following the latest developments. The lights from their screens illuminated their faces, highlighting their weary yet always focused eyes. One stark white charging line after another stretched across the floor, all winding together—everyone here was involved in a struggle that quickly drained their phones' power, so every plug always had a reliably warm iPhone charger attached to it.

Yang Jibin was hurrying over in a taxi. Just as he was approaching the Liede Bridge, Xiao Hua called and said, "You don't need to come. Sit down right now and write out everything that happened with this New Year's issue." Yang Jibin felt confused: "Didn't we arrange for people to write this up last night?" Xiao Hua responded, "Don't think too much, just do it."

What was to be done? That night in the "Losers" (*diaosi*) WeChat group, former *Southern Weekly* reporter Shen Liang sent an urgent message to colleagues: "We need external support. Don't worry anymore about potential reprisals, and don't hold on to any more illusions. It's possible that tomorrow an official inspection group could come in. Do you really think they couldn't foresee you going on strike?" Qin Xuan echoed, "Newspapers are already dying off; we really have no other options."

Despite the fear that he felt, Qin Xuan was still confident that he maintained a clear mind about the events around him. His stance was

"Since we've gone this far, let's keep going." He called Chen Mingyang to share insights from the WeChat group: "If we back down, this would mean that market-based media in China will face even greater pressures from the propaganda department in the coming years, even perhaps for another whole decade. We can sacrifice ourselves, but we can't back down. This is not just a problem for *Southern Weekly*. This is a defining moment for journalism in China."

Before he left for Guangzhou, Qin Xuan had reached a decision: "If colleagues in the Southern Media Group go on strike in our compound, but no one from *Southern Weekly* goes down, then I'll go. I must go." In reaching this decision, he couldn't help but feel anxious for his wife: "Going into direct conflict with the system, I know that I'll pay a real price, and so will my family."

Everyone at *Southern Weekly* was furious when the paper's Weibo account was commandeered. But unlike Qin Xuan, most calmed down eventually, and gradually set aside their more "extreme" impulses. Of course, in this process one issue always in the back of people's minds was the very real possibility of reprisals for further activism. In preparation for such potential worst-case scenarios, colleagues in the news department had set up a "four-hour safety reporting system," wherein everyone would type "checking in" in a WeChat group every four hours.

A few members of the editorial committee went to another room to hold a secret meeting in the middle of the night. Everyone else, with nothing to do, passed the time by sharing their thoughts on social media. One reporter suddenly shared, "My husband reassured me, if I lose my job, he'll support me." Soon thereafter, she saw another post in their WeChat group, "Haining's wife said to him, let's just not buy a car, let's save the three hundred thousand. That way, if things don't go according to plan, you won't have to work for a few years."

What were the worst-case scenarios running through people's minds at the time? I asked many people this question. Most responded that their worst-case scenario was losing their job at *Southern Weekly* or being unable to ever work in journalism again. Some people said that if they couldn't work in journalism anymore, they would be disappointed. I was surprised that almost no one voiced concerns about money. Of course, there were some who cautiously acknowledged that within their subconscious they hoped to keep this job, its income, and the respect that this position brought in the journalism industry. As they said, it was, all in all, a "pretty comfortable" job.

Cao Junwu also shared with me potential situations that he would have been unable to accept—creating problems for his family, or even losing his freedom. He half-jokingly added, "Please don't arrest me, I'm too much of a coward."

That night, some netizens posted on Weibo that they planned to go to the Southern Media compound in Guangzhou or the *Southern Weekly* offices in Beijing and Shanghai to show their support for the paper. Almost immediately, internal information from the regime's security services was leaked in the WeChat group: "The Public Security Bureau (PSB) has already drafted a response plan." A series of heated exchanges emerged almost immediately, with colleagues reminding one another of the stakes of any course of action.

Tian Lunan: Don't share posts about "taking walks" [note: a euphemism for demonstrations]!

Su Yongtong: Don't allow yourself to be used as a weapon by the enemy.

Kang Wangbei: "Frontal Command" recommends that everyone refrain from sharing, liking, or commenting on such posts.

Hong De: I recommend that the editorial committee immediately draft a new statement responding to the public's support and calling upon everyone to show their support in "reasonable" ways. This will help to wash our hands of any potential mass incidents tomorrow.

Su Yongtong: Important announcement: Dear colleagues, according to posts online, there is a possibility that people might gather tomorrow at the Southern Media Group headquarters and our various offices around the country, laying down flowers or engaging in other activities. Please refrain from any discussion of or any contact with these activities. Avoid any and all such interactions.

At 12:20 a.m. on January 7, an internal notice was posted in the WeChat group:

Southern Weekly embraces a long-standing tradition of compassion, justice, conscience, and reason. At this crucial moment, we continue to uphold our positive, forward-looking, balanced, and robust editorial style, tracing the trends of our times. Here at *Southern Weekly*, you read and understand China.

As news professionals, at this crucial moment we must defend our rights in a reasonable and restrained manner. We thus call on everyone to come together to defend our paper and our dignity. We are all in this together, for better and for worse.

1. Please do not accept interviews from overseas media.
2. Please do not post inflammatory or agitating comments. Refrain from using such phrases as "creating history" or "freedom of the press."
3. Please do not organize or encourage any other groups to get involved in this matter.
4. Please do not casually share any information under the *Southern Weekly* name that has not been approved by the editorial committee.
5. Please do not post, share, or voice support for any posts about a strike.
6. We affirm that we support the principle of the Party guiding the media.
7. Protecting yourself is protecting *Southern Weekly*.

January 7, 2013

A moment of collective silence briefly reigned in the hotel suite. Chen Mingyang put in his earphones, frowned slightly, and listened to his WeChat voice messages with a dour stare. Wu Chuanzhen wandered back and forth, his hands stuffed in his pockets. Shi Zhe pushed his reading glasses up to his temple, his eyes never wavering from his cellular phone screen. Su Yongtong sat swaying back and forth on the edge of the room's massive bed, his eyes noticeably red.

This was a long night in which many people, even beyond the small circle of *Southern Weekly* insiders, were also unable to sleep. Supporters of the paper were waiting to see what the next step would be, ready at any moment to share news of the latest developments. A friend called Liu Chang to ask when to expect further developments. Liu Chang responded, "All I can say is, soon. Don't sleep, trust me brother, don't go to sleep just yet."

It was 2:00 in the morning when Su Yongtong sent out a message that thrilled everyone who had been waiting.

Su Yongtong: Get ready everybody!! Get in place!

Tong Jingxi: Our attack is beginning.

Tian Lunan: Great, I'm waiting.

Li Shuifang: Here it is, great, I'm awake.

Xi Wan: Reporting!

Da Tongxin: Awaiting orders!

Nong Linxia: Get in place, whatever. . . . I'm on Sina Weibo.

Kang Wangbei: Putting on my work face, awaiting further orders.

At 2:26 a.m., Liu Chang finalized the text of the statement and saved it as an image file, which he then shared in the WeChat group. As if preparing for a rocket launch, he commented, "Comrades, take positions!" Some people had already shared the post when Liu Chang noticed a typo and added, "Oh, hold on a second."

Four minutes later, after completing his revisions, Su Yongtong issued the command, "Post now!" The details behind *Southern Weekly*'s official Weibo account being forced to publish Huang Can's intentionally deceptive explanation was shared by all staff whose Weibo accounts had not yet been shut down by the authorities, and immediately spread like wildfire. The conclusion to this post read as follows:

> While editorial staff at *Southern Weekly* are demanding that a thorough investigation be conducted into the changes to the New Year's issue, some people and groups have been deceptively talking themselves into circles, recklessly disregarding the facts, engaging in a conspiratorial plot to avoid looking into the matter, and employing administrative orders to distort the truth. We call on everyone to show respect for the truth, and to avoid any type of interference

before this investigation reaches its conclusion. Let's allow the truth
to be known and recorded for future generations.

We want to emphasize again: we support the principle of the
Party guiding the media, but resolutely oppose unreasonably invasive
management styles that violate normal journalistic and editing work.
Southern Weekly's staff is currently preparing an emergency investigative report on the events surrounding the New Year's issue. This
report will be released soon, to share the truth of this matter with
everyone!

That night, at least two colleagues passed on a recommendation from
friends inside the system: "Don't release the next issue." Some felt that
such advice was not in any way constructive, but discussion continued
about the possibility of at least delaying the next issue.

The third document in the drive to save *Southern Weekly* from
destruction was still being composed. Ju Jing and Zhu Hongjun, who
oversaw this process, didn't sleep the entire night. They remember
watching Wu Xiaofeng sitting alone in a little room in the suite, writing
out the details of the changes to the special issue made on January 2.
They were moved by his dedication.

The text went through a series of twists and turns. Colleagues had
their concerns about how frank Wu Xiaofeng would really be, fearing
that he might cover up some of the facts to make things easier for
himself. Wu Xiaofeng countered by arguing that he was actually risking
everything in order to share his account of these events, and that he
shouldn't be treated with such suspicion. Tensions built between Wu
and Chen Mingyang: Chen was focused on getting every little detail
exactly right, while Wu was eager to get the story down and released to
the public. Other members of the "Frontal Command" tended to sympathize with Wu's sense of urgency.

The sun had already risen by the time consensus was finally forced
on the narrative. Even then, a few people suddenly started to feel
uncertain again and demanded that additional evidence be provided for
a few claims; the atmosphere in the room grew tense. Eventually, Wu
Xiaofeng found text messages from the propaganda department official
on his phone, holding them up for all to see, while at the same time
never letting go of his phone.

After management confiscated the paper's Weibo account, Wu Xiaofeng suddenly became very eager to express himself. But this eagerness

only lasted for about twenty-four hours—I unfortunately completely missed it. After January 8, whenever I tried to enter his office suite to talk things over, he refused to let me in, with a hint of a smile.

Wu only ever provided a few brief comments to me: he wanted to emphasize that everything he did was for the good of the paper. He never did interviews, never made public comments on the web, and never used social media—indeed, once he left work, this deputy editor in chief from Zhejiang was nowhere to be seen.

Compared to Huang Can, Wu Xiaofeng had always been more concerned about what his colleagues thought of him. He liked to portray himself as a selfless man who made all types of sacrifices for the paper—even though his colleagues did not understand him, he did all he could in dealing with propaganda department officials in order to give *Southern Weekly* more space to do what it did best. "There have been times when I have perhaps yielded a bit too much, I'll admit, but I have never given in on my bottom line. It doesn't matter to me what my colleagues think of me, I have a clear conscience." Wu Xiaofeng wandered through the suite, with dark rings under his eyes, murmuring about his future, "You know, I'm done for."

Risking everything for the good of the paper? Wu's self-description did not always match what his colleagues saw.

Having joined *Southern Weekly* at its heyday, Wu Xiaofeng had written some outstanding investigative reports. But beyond his diligence in reporting, Wu did not exactly have the best reputation. Wu had a buzz cut, and beyond his black-rimmed glasses was a tiny pair of eyes that left his thoughts hidden to all. Wu was skilled in assessing situations and carefully weighing the pros and cons of any course of action. As a result, he had risen through the ranks at the paper, even amid one personnel shake-up after another. Some colleagues noted, jokingly, that even when *Southern Weekly* was losing, Wu Xiaofeng somehow always found a way to win.

When Zhang Dongming was placed behind the editorial desk at *Southern Weekly* by the Provincial Propaganda Department in 2003, he attempted to reshape the paper according to the demands of the propaganda department. For the first time in *Southern Weekly*'s history, its founding principle of a paper run by real journalists was lost. Also for the first time, many colleagues felt that a deputy editor in chief, Wu

Xiaofeng, far too often stood together with the paper's overseers, particularly Zhang Dongming.

Had propaganda officials not forcefully published this false statement on *Southern Weekly*'s Weibo account, there is no doubt that Wu Xiaofeng would have been standing together with Huang Can. But now, Wu realized, these officials with whom he had strived to cooperate and avoid all conflict over the years were determined to provoke conflicts to destroy *Southern Weekly*. Weren't they just using him as a scapegoat? Wu was not an idiot. When he realized that he was being used by the system, he regretfully yet resolutely changed course, refusing any longer to hide the names of the two provincial propaganda officials involved in these controversial edits.

On the morning of January 7, Zhu Hongjun saw Chen Mingyang casually making one phone call after another from his smoke-filled room. Zhu hurriedly interrupted: "Give me the phone. Check over what Wu Xiaofeng wrote, and post it." By 11:00 in the morning, "The Full Story of the Preparation and Publication of *Southern Weekly*'s 2013 New Year Special Issue" was finally posted online, including all the details narrated by Wu Xiaofeng.

Wu Xiaofeng's tendency to seek maximum advantage even in the worst of situations, once an object of criticism among colleagues, became a source of praise in this context. Facing a crisis, Wu had unsurprisingly chosen the path that would be most beneficial for him. But this time, he was not the only beneficiary; *Southern Weekly* as a whole also benefited from his shrewdness.

Wu Wei's announcement of the handover of the paper's official Weibo account and Zeng Li's public comments on the changes to the New Year's issue sent public opinion into an uproar. Then, the staff's joint statement, the public release of the details of the Weibo account's confiscation, and the detailed recounting of the changes to the special issue emerged, one after another, like a series of strikes against the deceptive official narrative of events at *Southern Weekly*.

Two versions of the "truth," one coming from officials, the other coming from the paper's staff, attempted to win over the public's trust. Young people witnessing what appeared to be the end of *Southern Weekly* gradually came to the realization that no one actually believed the official version of events.

Highly influential people in Chinese society began openly voicing their public support for *Southern Weekly*, including entrepreneur Lee Kai-fu, along with such movie stars as Yao Chen, Li Bingbing, and Chen Kun, each of whom have millions of followers on their microblog accounts.

In contemporary China, the rapid growth of new media has presented unprecedented challenges for rulers hoping to maintain their control over the flow of information. They may be able to invest seemingly infinite sums into building and reinforcing information blockades, but officials will never be able to overcome their own lack of familiarity with new technologies. For example, Guangdong Province had set up a high-level department tasked with internet management. Senior cadres outnumbered regular staff in this department's office. While these cadres had political power and connections, their grasp of new technologies was laughable: they might as well have been living in the stone age. They could not grasp even the fundamentals of Weibo. The development of these events at *Southern Weekly* was driven forward not only by journalists' use of new technologies, but also by officials' complete lack of understanding of these technologies.

11

HITTING A WALL

Beyond the windows, people rushed to work on Guangzhou's Siyou New Road the same as any other day. In the wee hours of the morning of January 7, the "Frontal Command" had determined its target: Huang Can. As Chen Mingyang put it: "*Southern Weekly* can live on, *Southern Weekly* will only get better. If we can't get rid of Tuo Zhen and his management style, at the very least we need to get rid of Huang Can."

First thing in the morning, Jiang Yiping hurried over to ask Yang Xingfeng, "How's everything?" Yang shared the news that Provincial Party Secretary Hu Chunhua had personally inquired about the situation at *Southern Weekly*. Yang Jian had also called to announce plans to hold a meeting at 10:30 a.m., bringing together editors and management to discuss some of the proposals put forward about changes to the prepublication review process and personnel.

Jiang Yiping was excited to hear this news. "I hurried to call everyone at *Southern Weekly*. But they had been in meetings all night, so most were still asleep. So I told Yang, 10:30 just isn't going to work, let's move the meeting to 3:30 p.m."

At noon, after just a few hours of sleep, leaders of the "Frontal Command" woke up energized by news of the meeting. You could even hear the occasional excited chuckle echo through their suite.

Wu Xiaofeng, Yuan Lei, Xiao Hua, and everyone involved had a look of energized expectation as they discussed, one by one, which demands they would raise in the meeting. Chen Mingyang took out his pen and paper, taking notes on each of the options considered by the "Frontal

Command," including a public, formal statement on the *Southern Weekly* situation, explaining this affair to the public; improving relations between the propaganda department and the media; requiring any and all limits on reporting to be enacted in accordance with central regulations, and requiring open responses to questions about these limits; granting the final approval on all publications to *Southern Weekly*'s editorial committee; removing Huang Can and bringing in a senior manager who understands *Southern Weekly*; and ending aggressive prepublication review. In this fleeting moment of optimism, they had even pondered pushing for the creation of a *Southern Weekly* Development Fund.

As the meeting time approached, colleagues began pacing the long and winding halls, chatting with members of the "Frontal Command" as they departed. Some joked, "If you are detained, I'll be sure to bring some fruit for you to snack on in prison." Everyone seemed relaxed. It was an overcast day, but rays of sunshine were shining through the clouds. People were feeling optimistic—this emotional roller coaster was, we might say, at its peak.

Ju Jing was chosen to stay back at the Golden Bridge Hotel to see how things developed. He was adamant that even if some colleagues were detained at the meeting, everyone shouldn't immediately go marching into the streets. Nevertheless, he was determined to make sure that any such developments be made public. That afternoon, Ju Jing was unable to hide his anxiety, constantly fidgeting. He would sit down abruptly with a thud in front of his computer, and then suddenly pick up and stare at his phone. At other times, he sat with both hands covering his face. Everyone awaited further news.

A little after three, Jiang Yiping stood at a window in the sixth floor of the compound's old building, looking nervously to the streets below. Occasionally, she would make a call to ask when everyone was arriving. Finally, the *Southern Weekly* representatives appeared. Yang Jibin and Cao Junwu came all the way in from Panyu. As always, they were late.

Some participants recorded the meeting for documentation, as well as sharing pieces of information with colleagues and supporters via WeChat while the meeting was in session.

The layout of the old office building was distinctive—shaped like a big boldface X. That day's discussion just happened to be held at the center, where the four wings came together. The windows, with their old black metal frames, were shut tightly, but the encouraging shouts of protesters still floated from the courtyard through the gently waving palm trees, all the way through to every corner of the awkwardly shaped 601 meeting room, mixing with the perpetually irreconcilable dialogue between the two sides. Supporters' chants continued until the sun had begun to fade. But as the meeting dragged on, Zhu Hongjun remembered feeling the cruelty of reality gradually dawning upon him. "I started to feel cold all over," he recounts.

Despite everyone's initial optimism, this was not a good afternoon for *Southern Weekly*. Elsewhere in town, public security officials had also been called for a meeting to notify them of the "verdict," meaning the state's official stance, on the *Southern Weekly* affair. In short, the state saw this as part of a broader ideological struggle, with foreign powers intervening to challenge the Party's bottom line on media control. The state-nationalist tabloid *Global Times* published a commentary the same day making the same points. And in Beijing, this same verdict was communicated to senior cadres in central state media outlets. Although none of this was known in the *Southern Weekly* meeting room at the time, the official stance quickly became apparent, shaping the tone of the dialogue that afternoon and crushing everyone's hopes.

The 601 meeting room is next door to Jiang Yiping's office. "I stood outside the door, listening on and off. I couldn't always hear what was being said," she remembers. Around four o'clock, she recalls, the discussion turned to the question of this official verdict. Yuan Lei commented that this official stance was not only bad for *Southern Weekly* but had deeper implications for all of Guangdong Province as a pioneer locality in the reform process. She asked that the provincial propaganda authorities do all that they could to push back against this official stance. Yang Jian replied that he would do his best.

Then, around 5:00, more bad news arrived: local newspapers had been ordered to carry the *Global Times* commentary, which claimed that the entire situation at *Southern Weekly* was the work of anti-China forces. At that point, standing outside of the meeting room, Jiang Yiping could hear everything very clearly—tempers and voices were rising on both sides.

Reflecting on this meeting afterward, participants told me that Yang Jian was a terrifyingly effective negotiator, with *Southern Weekly* representatives seeming immensely inexperienced by comparison. The fiery optimism that the paper's representatives had brought into the 601 meeting room disappeared quickly and completely. Yang Jian denied that there was any system blocking reports before they were written and did not even respond to the request for an official investigation into the incident. The editors' trump card seemed to be delaying publication of the next issue, but when they raised this possibility, Yang Jian seemed stunningly indifferent: If you skip an issue, go ahead, he said, I'll just say we're on break. If you stop work on one issue, I'll say we're taking a one-week break; two issues, I'll say we're on a two-week break. Anything more than that, I'll bring in some new people to write for me. Despite Yang's seeming nonchalance, the Central Propaganda Department had already ordered that *Southern Weekly* must continue publishing on schedule, so that nothing would seem amiss.

Southern Weekly's representatives felt that they had hit a wall. Yang Jian did not even accept the once seemingly inevitable removal of Huang Can, choosing instead to stall, saying that any change in personnel would need to be in accordance with regulations.

After the meeting, Yang Jibin felt that despite the outcome, they had done all that they could. Wu Wei felt in retrospect that everyone's expectations for this meeting were completely detached from reality. Seemingly reasonable and convincing proposals had in some cases been discussed for less than a minute before being dismissed. The young contributors to *Southern Weekly* were generally a lot savvier than others their age and tended to despise Party-talk and political tricks. They were confident that they had reached a higher understanding of political reality. But now, they could see that no matter how high one goes, there is no escaping this all-too-real and unyielding reality.

After Yang Jian departed, the *Southern Weekly* team invited Jiang Yiping in for a talk, to hear her opinion. Jiang said that she was in regular contact with Zuo Fang and Fan Yijin of the Southern Media Group, and that both agreed that *Southern Weekly* was the group's most valuable publication. Jiang reminded the paper's young contributors not to underestimate their negotiating power.

Jiang Yiping later told me that she regretted that the meeting had not started at 10:30 a.m. as originally scheduled. Had the meeting taken place before the "official verdict" was announced that afternoon, things might have turned out very differently. Jiang had been in touch throughout the day with Hu Shuli of Caixin Media, who was known for her fast talk and fast action. Hu promised that once an agreement had been reached between *Southern Weekly* contributors and management, Caixin would make it public immediately. As she said at the time, "Once we publish it, they can't take it back." But such an agreement was never reached.

As all this unfolded, Li Changchun, the recently retired head of the Central Propaganda Department, was visiting Guangdong, accompanied on his travels by Tuo Zhen. For those of us outside the inner circle of top officials, it is impossible to know whether the sudden hard-line shift that afternoon was in any way related to his visit.

A sense of insecurity reigned and cast suspicions everywhere: the eavesdropper, the spy among us, the ever-growing feeling of being surrounded. In order to avoid monitoring, at the start of meetings for the paper's economics department, everyone had to put their phones inside a closed metal box. Actually, no one had anything all that pressing or secret to discuss at these meetings. It was more of a formality whose purely symbolic value was demonstrated by the fact that any participants who arrived late and thus missed this opening ritual were never required to hand over their phones.

That night in the WeChat group, as some discussed whether the group was secure, Su Yongtong posted a report on the results of that afternoon's "clash":

> Notes from the January 7 meeting (for internal distribution only, not to be shared beyond this group)
> Our demands:
>
> 1. We demand that the Provincial Propaganda Department provide a verdict on this situation and promise that they will not seek revenge in the future upon anyone involved.
> 2. Implement a solely post-composition review system that does not screen topics in advance. All local matters should be handled in accordance with the Provincial Propaganda Department's standards, and matters covered elsewhere in China should be handled in accordance with the Central Propaganda Department's standards.
> 3. Implement a system wherein the editorial committee takes primary responsibility for content under the leadership of a general editor.

4. Remove Huang Can from his editor in chief position and replace him with a senior figure of integrity and repute who understands *Southern Weekly* and its values.

Since *Global Times'* commentary emerged during our negotiations, we specifically discussed how to respond to and resolve that issue in the latter part of our exchange.

Management promised:

1. They will not seek revenge on anyone involved.
2. They agreed to a system wherein the editorial committee takes primary responsibility for content, under the leadership of a general editor.
3. Any removal or replacement of employees must be done in accordance with regulations.
4. A final official verdict on this incident is not able to be reached immediately.
5. They promised to improve their management style.
6. There was a rumor that the Provincial Propaganda Department would announce an official verdict on this situation today, but they clarified that this was not in fact the case.
7. They will do all that they can to raise concerns about the *Global Times* commentary as soon as possible.

Both sides agreed that *Southern Weekly* is an influential media brand that deserves to be treated with respect. Both sides agreed to do all that they can to contribute to maintaining *Southern Weekly's* strength.

And finally, we must emphasize again: if you really love this newspaper, no leaks!

Colleagues who had been eagerly awaiting the outcome of this meeting, even skipping dinner to see what was happening, were greatly disappointed. Most of what management said seemed empty and meaningless. Some felt that there was already no chance of a fair resolution. The atmosphere in the WeChat group fluctuated between a sense of tragedy and a continued eagerness to encourage one another:

Chao Yin: We did all that we can; we did what was right.

Feng Puxi: Indeed. We have nothing to regret.

Tian Lunan: Reform through labor was already abolished. The worst that could happen is that we get detained a few days [grimacing].

After the meeting *Southern Weekly*'s representatives proceeded to a cramped Hunanese restaurant where colleagues awaited their arrival. Following Cantonese customs, everyone washed their plates and utensils in tea water, but as they fiddled with their silverware, the only thing on everyone's mind was the face-off that had just ended.

"I'm worried that we have been tricked again," Cao Junwu said despondently.

"Brothers, we have nothing. Our feet are bare and our wallets are empty. We have nothing to be tricked out of. . . . We laid our cards out on the table, four or five of them. No matter whether they go along with us or kill us off, we did what we needed to do. We were outmatched from the beginning, trying to face off against this giant superpower that crushes anything in its path. We never had a chance," Yang Jibin responded.

Yang Jibin reviewed the day's events and concluded that things were cooling down. He told colleagues, "We know that at some point in our confrontation with the authorities, *Southern Weekly* will have to back down. Nevertheless, we will survive. We can bang our heads against this hard wall, and even if all that is left is traces of our bloodstains on this wall, we will have won so long as those who come after us can still see those stains." Yang recounts, "Maybe this was an overly dramatic way to say it, but that's really how I felt at the time."

Shi Zhe shifted the discussion to Yang Jian's hard-line approach. Yang had claimed that if staff members went on strike, they would just announce that the paper was on break for one or two issues. But at the same time, he said that no one could release details of this dialogue publicly. Such comments were oddly contradictory, combining a seeming arrogant nonchalance and an insecure anxiety for control. Cao Junwu felt that the management's repeated declarations that they were not scared of a strike actually showed that they were terrified of this possibility.

"Well then let's give it a try," said Yang Jibin.

"All that we can really do at this point is sit back and watch. It's all beyond us." International media later reported that even Chairman Xi

Jinping was at this moment seeking more information about what exactly was happening at *Southern Weekly*.

As the aroma of dried red peppers floated through the air, a few reporters wondered whether they owed an account of the meeting and its outcomes to netizens. Perhaps, they added, they could put together some materials and find a way to get them to Beijing. Cao Junwu responded, "We are just little fish. Any attempt we make to swim away will be futile and will only further muddy the waters."

12

A REAL SOCIAL MOVEMENT

"Go ahead, film me."

A young woman known online as Miss Ranxiang distributed forty-nine chrysanthemum flowers to the people standing around her, before stepping forward to place one last flower at the front entrance of the 289 Guangzhou Avenue Southern Media Group compound. As she turned around to walk back, facing the policemen filming her, she removed her mask to show that she had no intention of hiding her identity. Her mask covered her mouth not to disguise her, but to embody the regime's infringement of citizens' freedom of expression. She had no need to hide, as she was even prepared to be arrested—she had a warm sweater and some toiletries in her backpack in anticipation of her likely detention.

While some hesitated to accept her flowers, Miss Ranxiang's courage was gradually infectious, leading ever more people to lay flowers at the entrance to the Southern Media Group compound. Gradually, some supporters who had just been standing and watching from the sidelines began to leave behind their fears, gathering and shouting slogans in support of free speech. From around noon on January 7, ever more people joined, brought together in anger at the confiscation of the paper's Weibo account. At the protest's peak, hundreds stood in front of the Southern Media Group compound.

Miss Ranxiang was not the first person to take a public stand in support of *Southern Weekly*. On January 5, Shen Ge, a chef in Guangzhou, came to stand in solitary protest outside the compound with a sign that read, "*Southern Weekly* staff are heroes, down with Tuo Zhen." Police had arrived within ten minutes, advising him that since he had made his views clear, it was time to move along. He resisted and was able to remain standing in protest for another ten minutes.

Shen Ge wanted to promote a different vision of protest—protest that wasn't all doom and gloom, but that rather celebrated the potential for optimism. Miss Ranxiang said the same of her protest—we don't want to be so somber; we want to keep things exciting. Performance artist Qu Zhihang also took a memorable selfie from across Guangzhou Avenue—in the nude, he did a push-up facing *Southern Weekly*'s neon advertising billboard.

An even more unique approach to protest was reported in Shenzhen. Du Yinghong, an artist, wrapped a torn copy of *Southern Weekly* around his head and moaned and groaned as he made his way to Bao'an Hospital for treatment. When filling out his intake forms, under *symptoms* he wrote, "Feeling pain all over, my brain refuses to follow orders."

Then, on the afternoon of January 7, a self-proclaimed "little socialist warrior" came to share his leftist thinking with protestors gathered outside the compound, starting arguments here and there. The stretch of sidewalk in front of the paper's offices became ever more lively, as the roar of bus engines and the blare of car horns mixed with calls for freedom of the press, recitations of the thirty-fifth article of the PRC constitution, calls to "express yourself reasonably, stay calm," and curses of "you dumb cunts," coming together to form an intoxicating cacophony. At that moment, the police force's main priority was maintaining order, politely telling protestors, "Please work with us while we fulfill our duties."

Protestors sang songs that recounted the Formosa Incident in Taiwan. This historic event had many parallels with the *Southern Weekly* situation: under martial law, the Taiwanese journal *Formosa* was closed in 1979 for its discussion of such sensitive topics as human rights. Yet beyond these immediate, obvious parallels, we must also remember that the Formosa Incident eventually became a turning point in Taiwan's transition from a dictatorship to a democracy, kicking off a decade of activism that led to Taiwan's political liberalization.

The not-so-invisible hand that had grabbed *Southern Weekly*'s Weibo account also unintentionally pushed the paper's supporters onto the streets. After a couple of days of back-and-forth online, people angered by these developments opted for this most traditional form of protest, with supporters showing up with signs and flowers not only at *Southern Weekly*'s offices in Guangzhou, but also in Beijing, Shanghai, and Chengdu.

In the deserted offices of *Southern Weekly*'s Guangzhou headquarters on January 7, Qin Xuan encountered a soft-spoken young woman who had somehow managed to find her way inside. At first, she said she had come to apply for a job, but then she suddenly started crying. Qin Xuan could tell that she was a young supporter who was worried for *Southern Weekly* but did not know how to express her feelings. As they talked, Qin learned that she was a second-year student at the Guangdong University of Finance and Economics. He gave her some tissues and water to drink.

Fang Kecheng also encountered a silent supporter in the hallway outside the Beijing office. He was around thirty and stood steady outside the office's glass doors, refusing to speak and refusing to leave.

Around 2:00 a.m. on January 9, Ye Weimin also ran into a young man holding a sign voicing his support for *Southern Weekly* on a pedestrian crossover. He explained to Ye that he was busy at work during the day, so he could only find time to come out and make his voice heard at night.

For a week after January 7, more than twenty police cars remained parked in the rear courtyard behind the Southern Media Group compound at all times. But in the first three days of protests, the police had clearly received orders to take a more measured approach. Day after day, reporters from dozens of international news agencies gathered with hundreds of supporters, as speeches were made, slogans were shouted, debates were held, and songs were sung. Supporters' and critics' voices made their way unrestrained through the chilly winter air.

At no point were any reports on these protests carried by Chinese media.

How to get these *Southern Weekly* editors talking? This question was on the minds of every international journalist standing outside of the Southern Media Group compound. Yet no one was able to make any progress. All too familiar with the sinking feeling that comes from hearing "no comment," many contributors to *Southern Weekly* nevertheless found themselves saying, "Sorry, no comment" dozens of times a day to fellow journalists.

With protests moving from the virtual world onto the streets, *Southern Weekly* began to attract more international attention. The spokesperson for the US Department of State voiced concerns, as did several Taiwanese political figures; everyone called for China to relax its controls on the media. Temperatures continued to rise, and propaganda officials continued to add timber to this growing fire. There seemed to be no turning back.

Everyone affiliated with *Southern Weekly* was given repeated internal warnings: don't go outside, and definitely don't join in any protests. Cutting themselves off completely from external supporters was not in fact a new approach. *Southern Weekly* contributors had always taken great care to avoid any appearance of associating with supporters in civil society, particularly with supporters abroad. They always strove to draw a clear line, keeping their distance from protests or political activities. This caution, as well as repeated declarations that they were not attempting to challenge the Party's control over media, grew out of a certain familiarity with how the Party responds to crises.

We can also see similar caution among the protestors in Beijing in 1989, who were also all too familiar with how the Party handled such situations. Student protestors held signs with slogans like "Resolutely support the Party's correct leadership," and kept their distance from supporters in broader society for quite some time. A most disgraceful manifestation of this approach was the decision to hand over three young men from outside of Beijing to public security after they threw black ink at the image of Mao Zedong on the Tiananmen rostrum. Protestors even met with the press at the time to distance themselves from this deeply evocative act of protest.

Although both faced a common adversary, the demands put forward in Guangzhou in 2013 were quite different from those raised in Beijing in 1989. And one could even say that the demands put forward by *Southern Weekly* staff in 2013 were quite different from the demands expressed by their supporters. At the end of the day, the people involved with *Southern Weekly*, or at least most of them, just wanted to see an improvement in their working and thus living conditions; they also hoped to see the officials who had been tormenting them punished.

Any greater aspirations could only find a voice among the supporters gathered outside the compound.

He Qinglian, a Chinese scholar living in exile, penned a commentary on the *Southern Weekly* affair, characterizing the protests as "a clear expression of intellectuals' and the middle class's yearning for political rights." The significance of this event, as He pointed out, went far beyond the very limited scope within which *Southern Weekly* contributors framed it. Both main actors in this affair, namely the staff of *Southern Weekly* and the Chinese Communist Party, spared no effort in dodging the real issue here: state control of the press and the desire for freedom.

A netizen writing under the pen name Nianhua Commentaries posted excerpts from a protestor's speech delivered in Guangzhou on January 8, which read, "We have fought for our interests, fought for more benefits, fought for land, and fought for a home. But this is the first time that we are truly fighting for our freedom!" To be more precise, one could say that this was the first time since 1989 that people truly fought for their freedom.

On a typical day outside of the 289 Compound, you would see several express couriers waiting for *Southern Weekly* staff to step out and pick up their parcels, coming and going. But now, instead of couriers, the area outside of the compound was occupied by crowds of protestors who showed no signs of leaving anytime soon.

On the afternoon of January 8, an employee of *Southern Metropolis Daily* watched a beige Toyota mini-bus with the label "Baiyun People's Government" stop in front of the Southern Media Group compound. About a dozen people got off carrying images of Mao and signs that read, "Down with this traitorous media group." They lined up at the entrance to the compound, adding yet another voice to the protests outside.

Southern Weekly journalists observing all this noticed that this new batch of protestors appeared to be not so well-off. Had the state hired some part-time workers to complicate matters even further? Sharing these suspicions, some *Southern Weekly* supporters began waving cash in front of these new arrivals, mocking their "activism."

I chose to speak with one of the participants who looked most like your average worker and eventually found myself engaged in an hour-long chat with him. At one point during our chat, he picked up a call and shouted loudly to the caller on the other end, "These traitors are simply out of their minds!"

The person with whom I spoke was indeed a migrant worker from the countryside. His specialty was home renovation. He told me that he and his fellow protestors came from an online chat group that embraced Mao Zedong Thought, and that they had mobilized and organized on their own. He claimed that the Southern Media Group "despised the Cultural Revolution" and had even raised doubts about Bo Xilai's policy of singing red songs and striking against black forces in Chongqing. He had thus asked for two days' leave from work to protest the traitors at *Southern Weekly*.

"My brothers and sisters back at home, we regular people, we just want to make some money to raise our families. Why did Chairman Mao launch the Cultural Revolution? He wanted to change the slave mentality of the Chinese people." He told me that he had been born in Hubei in 1976, the year that Mao died. Yet his life experiences had led him to develop ever-deeper feelings for this leader whom he described as "the type of sage that only emerges once every five thousand years." I must admit that I found it extremely difficult to follow his logic. Nevertheless, he was eager to share:

> In the Maoist era, we would never wander so far away from our parents, and never view money as our main aspiration in life. In the Maoist era, people were happy. Basically, family and friends stayed together, and whenever someone had a problem, people would be there to help. Nowadays, no matter what you do, even just moving some furniture, no one will step forward to help unless you pay them. . . . You need to understand the one and only way to truly save China. Mao's Cultural Revolution is the greatest manifestation of freedom and democracy. Kicking out the Party Committees and pressing forward with the revolution, could there be anything freer and more democratic than that? . . . *Southern Metropolis Daily* [author's note: he meant to say *Southern Weekly*] is also involved in a Cultural Revolution, as the people below are rebelling against those above them. But their Cultural Revolution is a bourgeois Cultural Revolution, the type that running dogs of the American imperialists would engage in. A real Cultural Revolution should focus its struggle on serving the broad masses of peasants and workers.

At this point in his monologue, competing chants of "fifty cent party" and "US running dogs" roared behind him. One participant who stood out in the crowd of Maoists was a middle-aged woman with short hair and a booming voice that made her excited thoughts all too clear to everyone present. As I watched her, she raised her arms in the air and shouted, "Long live the Chinese Communist Party!" and "Long live Chairman Mao!" For a brief second, I thought I had been transported back in time to the Cultural Revolution.

All the Maoists shouted the exact same slogans. Despite their unity, however, they did not seem any more energized than the diverse group of *Southern Weekly* supporters with their cornucopia of slogans and ideas. Police separated the two groups, placing them on either side of the compound's entrance to avoid the possibility of conflict; this, however, had the unintended effect of creating an even stronger sense that the two groups were facing off against each other.

Although this gathering outside of the Southern Media Group compound involved only a hundred or so, it felt more like a real social movement than anything participants had experienced in their lives. People were coming up with new and innovative ideas to voice their dissatisfaction. One scholar standing among the onlookers shared his recommended strategy with a *Southern Weekly* reporter: a high-profile reporter should quit the paper as a way of generating attention and support. Another supporter, the author Rou Tangseng, came up with the idea of selling a short story of his online to support any employees of *Southern Weekly* who lost their jobs. His story, memorably, consisted of only two words: "thank you." In the end, these ideas remained only that: ideas.

A real change in the situation arrived on January 10, when a few gardeners showed up with hoses to spray water over the flowerpots that adorned the sidewalk in front of the compound, along with the sidewalk itself. Their incessant spraying prevented people from standing in front of the compound, and in concert with the police, they managed to clear out all of the protestors. Even curious passersby were hurried away.

Before that moment, only plainclothes policemen had been involved in applying pressure on the protests by following, pulling aside, and interrogating *Southern Weekly* supporters. Liu Yimu and three of his friends, who had come all the way from Changsha to show their support, faced this form of intimidation. Liu had once worked in media and

believed that it was necessary at this point in China's history for everyone to push for genuine freedom of the press: "We need to stand up
and make our voices heard." As he and his friends left the area outside
of the Southern Media compound, fellow protestors notified them that
they were being followed. Eventually, with the protection and support
of other protestors, Liu and his friends were able to make their way
back to Changsha safely.

A wheelchair-bound petitioner had also been involved in the protests and had spoken with several international media organizations
over the past few days. Suddenly, four policemen surrounded him,
lifted him out of his wheelchair, and tossed him directly into a police
van waiting for him. The only way he could fight back was through his
screams. Some supporters were detained briefly at the site of the protests and beaten in custody. Miss Ranxiang and other relatively high-
profile supporters waited at home for the police to come and interro-
gate them.

Two months after these events, Liu Yuandong, who had held up
signs and given speeches outside No. 289, was detained by Guangzhou
police on suspicion of "gathering a crowd to disrupt order in a public
place" and "false declaration of registered capital." As 2013 ended, the
Tianhe District Procuratorate's charges against Liu were revealed online (Tianhe Procuratorate charges [2013] 2242), and his lawyer confirmed that Liu's case would be proceeding to trial. *Southern Weekly*
employees again faced a nagging yet fundamentally unanswerable question—how could they ever face protestors who literally risked everything to support them?

A few remembered that Yang Jian had promised that there would be
no retribution against *Southern Weekly* staff and their supporters. The
great efforts that had gone into securing this empty promise were far
from enough to calm the consciences of *Southern Weekly* staff.

Many major websites in China also showed their support in a variety
of ways; some included subtly hidden messages of support for *Southern
Weekly* in their headlines. Some sites' official censors even joined in the
fun, taking their precious time deleting related "sensitive" content; delaying a required deletion by ten or twenty minutes meant that more
people could see these stories. Such intentional sabotage disappointed
the internet management departments, which had backdoor entries

into every website that allowed them to delete content on their own—an ability they had to use multiple times as these events unfolded.

The state's refusal to budge brought people together. As online commentator Zhao Chu stated, "This newspaper brought together the hopes of a large group of people in the general public who want our media to promote positive change and real hope, as well as many journalists who hope to realize their ideals of journalism serving society rather than the state."

Alongside the response online, the paper also saw more "traditional" expressions of support—letters to the editor. Cai Junjian, the editor responsible for communicating with the paper's readers, chose a few letters of support that came from people "within the system" to share with and encourage his colleagues. Some excerpts include:

> I saw the latest developments about your New Year Message on Weibo. Is this really happening? I'm very worried that my favorite newspaper could be shut down. Fighting with those types of people, well, it's impossible to win. I hope that everyone at *Southern Weekly* stays strong! I support you! (XXX, a cadre in the Rugao Municipal Party Committee, Jiangsu Province)

❀ ❀ ❀

> What I read online about your New Year special issue really is disappointing. I wish you all the best. (XXX, head of a local administration of industry and commerce)

❀ ❀ ❀

> Why has there been so much talk about your New Year commentary? Did you say that our nation's political reform is stalled? I have also read that the Provincial Propaganda Department has demanded that you not print a story on Wang Lijun, as well as shutting down stories on some other sensitive topics—our country seems to be returning to more hard-line policies, while still claiming to be "reforming." I for one hope that in 2013 we will all have more space for democratic participation! (XX, head of the Food and Drug Administration in the XX district of Wenzhou, Zhejiang Province)

❀ ❀ ❀

As we welcome a new year, *Southern Weekly* shows again that it is not scared of cruel power politics and shared the most genuine of cries that has been building up in the hearts of the people for so long. I truly admire your work and will always support *Southern Weekly*! Never lose your pride, or your backbone! (XX, from the Press Room at the official Xinhua News Service)

❄ ❄ ❄

The people standing together with *Southern Weekly* were all too aware of the risks that they were facing. Nevertheless, they made their choice—to take action. One contributor to *Southern Metropolis Daily* described the difficulty of this type of decision on his Weibo account:

Why are we all so silent? Because this is an era in which one phone call can lead to you being fired. Because you need to have a home and provide for your family and go on living your life. Because your resistance could implicate those above and below you in the hierarchy. Because it could even lead to the closure of the entire paper. The only reason we are able to stand up today and make our voices heard in this moment is that the situation has reached a point that we simply can no longer bear. Because we are all in this together. Because there is a sword dangling over the heads of each and every one of us who works in media, and we never know when it will swing down at us. Because we know that anyone who fights for freedom and justice will never be alone.

A former colleague who had just started a new magazine and was thus all too familiar with the dual challenges of raising capital for media and dodging the restraints of censorship left the following comment on WeChat for colleagues at *Southern Weekly*: "When signing the petition and engaging in other activism surrounding this incident, I really hesitated. At some points, I couldn't even make up my mind. You see, my current financial situation is a bit difficult. But in the end, passion overrode reason. I know all too well the struggles that go into any decision. So, all that I can do is be myself and listen to my heart. No matter what happens to me, I will never regret what I did. I have faith in the future, faith that flowers will eventually bloom in the warmth of spring."

13

THE *BEIJING NEWS* DILEMMA

During the January 7 meeting, Yang Jian had promised he would do all that he could to raise staffers' concerns about the *Global Times* editorial. There was, however, not much that he could really do. This editorial and the official orders to reprint it added fuel to the already raging fires of the *Southern Weekly* affair.

Global Times, a subsidiary of the *People's Daily*, is a rare example of a largely market-based (but still state-controlled) paper openly thriving on populist nationalist agitation. Its editor, Hu Xijin, is a smooth-talking nationalist who loves to point out endlessly that "China is complex."

On the morning of January 4, *Global Times* carried an editorial titled "We Need Cool Heads to Deal with the *Southern Weekly* Incident," providing a revealing specimen of Hu's style of logic. "From time to time, in China's media management system, the state gives specific orders to media on important reports. Generally speaking, though, news reporting in China is becoming ever more open, and general trends indicate that the state is giving fewer direct orders to media." This commentary did not comment directly on whether interference in the media was right or wrong, but it certainly hinted that the time was not right for the type of resistance that was coming from *Southern Weekly*. Yet at the same time, Hu seemed eager to avoid getting on the bad side of *Southern Weekly* supporters, adding, "This event presents a serious challenge to the current media management system. The reality seems to be that the old system of media management cannot simply continue without adjustments. Our media management system needs to develop in step with the times."

Hu's commentary succeeded in annoying everyone from *Southern Weekly* supporters to the regime. But at the end of the day, it was the regime that *Global Times* really needed to worry about. Propaganda officials had ordered the commentary erased from the internet before 9:00 that morning. Another journalist who frequents the Central Propaganda Department confirmed to me that Hu had been sternly reprimanded.

Having failed in their first attempt, on the morning of January 7, the *Global Times* published a second commentary on this incident that read quite differently from the first. Its title was "*Southern Weekly's* Weibo Post Really Makes Us Think." After quoting from the statement posted on the paper's official Weibo account, the commentary stated, "This post on their official Weibo clearly explains how this situation emerged: a story completely different from the version that has been circulating online the last few days. Furthermore, according to *Global Times's* own contacts with relevant officials, the final front-page text was in fact not written by officials at the Guangdong Provincial Propaganda Department, as some have claimed."

This was a far more skillful attempt at "refuting rumors" than the previous attempt by Singapore's *Lianhe Zaobao*. Reading closely between the lines, we can begin to see the motives behind this commentary:

> This *Southern Weekly* turmoil has been building up for the past few days. But if you look at the situation carefully, you'll notice that the people most aggressively sharing information on this event online, other than those still working at the paper, are a number of people who stopped working at *Southern Weekly* a long time ago and no longer have any relationship with the paper, along with some activists on Weibo. In reality, these people are dispersed, and can only come together online. Their newest vocal supporter is none other than Chen Guangcheng, who lives all the way on the other side of the world, in the United States.
>
> The demands put forward by these activists are very extreme. At first glance, it might seem that they are responding to a specific event with which they are unhappy, but one can see that their real target is in fact the entire system of media management.

❀ ❀ ❀

Even in the West, mainstream media will not engage in open conflict with the government. Anyone who dares to engage in such conflict in China will be sure to lose. For a long time now there have been some peripheral figures who have tried to encourage some Chinese media organizations to engage in conflict with the state. But all they are really doing is digging a grave and inviting these media organizations to jump in.

❀ ❀ ❀

Some people love nothing more than excitement. If the media begin to openly resist the current system of media management, the resulting conflict would be much more "fun" to watch than any of the environmental mass incidents in Shifang or Qidong. If one media organization followed this path, and even succeeded, that would indeed be a fun development in these people's eyes and would fill their minds with all types of overexcited political reveries.

But in the end, none of these dreams are real, because in Chinese society today there is no popular support for this type of behavior. Everyone is focused on economic opportunities and improving people's livelihoods. There is no interest in injecting uncertain variables into the country's future, and everyone worries that any such change could wreck their peaceful lives.

In a truly unstable society, if someone were to self-immolate, or to engage in a small protest, or even share rumors online, any of these acts could be the start of something much bigger. But the real China is developing at breakneck pace and undergoing perpetual reforms. That China where "something big is about to happen" only exists in the minds of a few people on Weibo.

❀ ❀ ❀

I hope that everyone who cares about *Southern Weekly* will work together to cool down this disturbance. Don't push a Chinese newspaper to take on the role of the resistance: that's a burden far too heavy for them to bear.

It was no surprise to *Southern Weekly* staff that *Global Times* published a commentary that corresponded perfectly to the state's stance on this incident. What else, after all, would one expect? But then on the evening of January 7, news broke in the WeChat group that all major media outlets in China had been ordered to reprint this commentary. At first, everyone thought this had to be a joke, that it couldn't possibly be true. But eventually, after verification from multiple sources, it became a reality.

The authorities, it seems, were also not 100 percent sure what to make of this commentary: *Global Times* staff revealed that on the morning of January 7 the State Council Information Office responsible for internet monitoring had issued an order that the commentary be taken down. Then, just two hours later, they ordered every major news portal to reprint the same commentary.

Southern Weekly staff could see very clearly from the media outlets selected to carry the report that this was not just an attempt at manufacturing public opinion—this was an open assault by the state on the independence of market-based media, a declaration that media could never be anything more than regime mouthpieces. On the evening of January 7, many print media outlets did their duty by reprinting the commentary. A few managed to subtly show their dissatisfaction—some edited out a few sections, while others placed the commentary in a less-than-prominent location, and still others highlighted the characters for "reprint" to emphasize to readers that their own staff did not write this piece. Everyone knew whose view a required reprint represented.

As *Southern Weekly* staff shared various outlets' reprints among themselves, the power disparities in this struggle became ever more apparent. Deng Ke told me that he felt there was a massive net that had surrounded all his colleagues, leaving them with nowhere to run. He wished that he were a wealthy man, "so that I could just give every one of them three hundred or five hundred thousand a year, providing a space for these awesome journalists to do what they do best, far away from the disgraces they were facing on a daily basis."

Papers in the Southern Media Group naturally refused to carry this commentary. Standing together with them, *Beijing News* and Hunan's *Xiaoxiang Morning Paper* also refused. Such refusals earned these papers respect from their colleagues and wrath from officials.

Beijing News initially began as a collaboration between the Southern Media Group and the Guangming Daily Media Group. Because the paper embraced the same journalistic principles as other Southern Media papers, it repeatedly angered the propaganda authorities. Eventually, control of the paper was taken away from both the Southern and Guangming groups and handed over to the Beijing Municipal Propaganda Department.

After failing to get *Beijing News* and *Xiaoxiang Morning News* to carry this reprint on January 7, top officials applied pressure again on January 8 via local propaganda authorities. But journalists at both outlets were ready to resist. *Beijing News* put up the most dramatic resistance.

A little after 8:00 p.m. on the evening of January 8, a man with gray hair and frameless glasses entered the editorial offices of the *Beijing News*. This was Yan Liqiang, the deputy director of the Beijing Municipal Propaganda Department, who had come to personally ensure that the *Beijing News* would carry the *Global Times* commentary. Countless phone calls had thus far been unable to sway the paper's editors.

A lengthy back-and-forth proceeded behind the glass doors of the paper's meeting room. Reporters and editors could see all too clearly the somber looks on the faces of both sides of the exchange. *Beijing News*'s publisher Dai Zigeng and editor in chief Wang Yuechun clearly voiced their refusal to reprint the commentary, saying that they would both quit if required to do so. The debate went on into the middle of the night. When Yan Liqiang finally left well past 1:30 a.m., he again emphasized the authorities' resolve on this matter. According to Cheng Yizhong, a former editor in chief at *Beijing News*, the authorities had even sent armed police to watch over the print room.

As ever more reporters gathered at the paper's offices to watch this unfold, Dai Zigeng surveyed everyone's opinions. The result was unanimous: literally not even one journalist supported publishing the commentary. But then an order came down from above: that day's issue would not be printed unless it featured the commentary. Further resistance, superiors hinted, might result in the paper's closure. Silence fell over the hundreds gathered in the paper's offices.

A knife was figuratively being held to their throats. The rush of emotions felt as a result was shared live on the net. Censors were eager to delete images of *Beijing News* journalists standing together in tears, but their deletions were unable to keep up with the speed with which these images were shared. The flames started by the *Southern Weekly* incident grew to a point where they began to engulf the very heart of the Chinese state.

The Chinese state's censorship system had always operated largely behind the scenes. In this chain of events in early 2013, from the interference in the New Year's commentary to the confiscation of *Southern Weekly*'s Weibo account, onward to the *Beijing News* crisis, the shadow of this typically hidden censorship system could suddenly be seen clearly everywhere. A chain of events like this had never occurred in modern Chinese media.

When someone stands together with you in your struggle, refusing to back down despite the very real threat of repercussions, do you praise their courage and encourage them to continue, or for their own safety do you try to convince them to step back and keep silent? No matter one's choice, there was no right answer for *Southern Weekly* staff members facing the dilemma of how to respond to events unfolding at the *Beijing News*. Many felt that this situation was far more complex than any decisions they had ever faced—this was no longer just about themselves; others were now implicated. The debate in the paper's WeChat group that evening bore testament to these complications.

> Tong Jiheng: I'm starting to feel that maybe it's best that we don't say anything on this matter. We still haven't even resolved our own situation, so it's probably best to wait, right?
>
> Qin Xuan: We are facing real challenges, and others are stepping forward and standing up for us. But then, as a result, they are getting wrapped up in all our problems. We can't just sit back and pretend that nothing happened.
>
> Tong Jiheng: But if we speak up for them right now, will that help?
>
> Su Yongtong: What can we do to show our support?
>
> Nonglin Xia: No matter how we do it, we need to show our support for *Beijing News*.

Chen Mingyang met in his office with Cao Junwu, Yuan Lei, and others to brainstorm how to respond to this dilemma. He also asked the We-

Chat group, via Yuan Lei's account, what they thought: "Should we advise *Beijing News* to just go ahead and print this commentary?"

Five or six people agreed that this was probably the best option. Two minutes later, Su Yongtong sent a notification to everyone in the group: "Please call everyone you know at the *Beijing News* right now and tell them to just go ahead and print the commentary. We can't let our own troubles create any more problems for our brothers and sisters at *Beijing News*."

> Nonglin Xia: Pouring cold water on this: do you really think this is a good idea? Isn't there a chance they'll just laugh at this proposal, as will others?
>
> Shangdu: I disagree with this proposal. Please don't make this request in *Southern Weekly*'s name. Anyone who does so, know that I won't forgive you.
>
> Cao Junwu: At this moment of crisis, we can't just stand by and let our friends take a bullet for us.
>
> Shangdu: People are making sacrifices to stand up for you, and you're telling them to just obey orders. Do you really think they'll be grateful?
>
> Cao Junwu: Well, am I supposed to just stand by and watch them make these sacrifices then?!
>
> Chen Tianbei: I agree with Shangdu. And I also feel that any interference from us won't be helpful. After all, they are protesting the government's rape of their paper.
>
> Yuan Lei: But we can't just stand here and watch them as they are dragged off to the execution grounds.

Yang Jibin had worked at *Beijing News* and still knew people who worked there. Chen Mingyang asked Yang to give Dai Zigeng a call to encourage him to reprint the commentary, to avoid any further complications. In a brief exchange, Yang reassured Dai that no matter if they carried the commentary or not, they would always be brothers. Yang also passed along Chen Mingyang's request that the two speak directly, and Dai voiced no opposition. However, not long after they hung up, Yang received a message from someone inside the Party Committee at *Beijing News* encouraging him to stop Chen from making this call. There were two reasons: first, this call would leave both with very difficult choices, and second, it was essential to avoid any appearance of conspiring with one another.

Soon enough, news that the *Beijing News* staff had abandoned their fight reached Guangzhou, bringing an end to this ethical dilemma. A reminder was shared in the WeChat group: our discussion of these matters must never be made public.

Later, a *Southern Weekly* reporter had a chance to see an internal note that Wang Yuechun sent to the *Beijing News* staff, which read as follows.

Some basic facts that everyone needs to know:

1. Dai Zigeng has not resigned. If his resignation could help avoid the shame of reprinting this commentary, he would have resigned immediately.
2. The Beijing Municipal Propaganda Department is not responsible for this decision and has no room for maneuver: they are also being forced to do this.
3. *Beijing News* doesn't have any grandiose hopes about supporting anyone or changing anything. We just want to maintain our own space and dignity and keep our team and its aspirations together.
4. No matter what may happen, no one has the right to deny another person their livelihood.

Jiang Yiping received an emotional text message from Wang Yuechun: "The media is unable to report the news. Instead, we have become the news. This is a real tragedy."

For Yang Jibin, these decisions on the evening of January 8 were the most painful moment in this entire saga. He felt an unprecedented sense of despair, even greater than the night that the paper's Weibo account was confiscated. "This is the type of ethical dilemma they should feature in textbooks. If I don't make this call, there's no excuse; I'm forcing a friend to take a bullet for me. But if I do make the call, I turn myself into a martyr, while also belittling my friend's integrity."

Yang Jibin's wife had been a reporter for *Beijing News*, and they both had a deep affection for this paper. During this crisis, Yang Jibin talked with Cao Junwu on the phone for over an hour. He could tell that Cao was crying. They agreed that if anyone resigned from *Beijing News*, they would also resign from *Southern Weekly*.

Cao Junwu recounted that night as a real low point in this process: "An old guy who works in the steamed buns department can always tell everyone how to steam their buns, no problem. But now all of a sudden his responsibility is catching tigers. Do I have the qualifications to tell people how to catch tigers?"

Chen Mingyang told me that he also had conflicted feelings, although perhaps not quite as conflicted as Yang Jibin's.

> I respected *Beijing News*'s choice, whatever it would be. My basic assessment of the situation was that we were focused on relying on popular support in this fight, but what we really needed was support from a central leader. This entire affair could have been used by those in power to push for a more open media environment, but in the end they didn't. As for myself, I did not want the stability-maintenance wing of the party to have any other excuses to further expand their power. We needed to move beyond only seeing things through the framework of right versus wrong. There were far greater issues at stake.

At *Southern Weekly*, people liked to refer to each other affectionately as "teachers (*laoshi*)." To highlight Chen Mingyang's special status among the paper's many teachers, people called him "headmaster." Chen's long, puffy hair was his trademark, but it was already considerably shorter than the long, flowing locks he had in college in the 1980s, at Wuhan University. At that time, Chen had felt he was a solitary soul. He was fairly vain at the time and, in his own words, "was a bit of a showoff." From his time in university, Chen had concluded that the true pinnacles of human civilization could be summarized in just one line: freedom, love, democracy, and rule of law. These are "what make humans what they are." In the political context of China, a student with thoughts like Chen's was bound to be considered a "bad student."

But Chen Mingyang never acted rashly. His time in college overlapped with the 1989 democracy movement. He went around to various universities copying the contents of big-character posters and protest signs, recording people's comments, trying to get a sense of what the students were thinking, and then analyzing these trends with his friends. As he later told me, "Relatively speaking, I'm the type of person who prefers to sit back and witness history. I certainly won't charge forward immediately to join in."

As he talks, Chen likes to lightly tap his feet on the ground. He is not an impulsive person, and his style of speech matches his demeanor. Occasionally, he will cast his sight out beyond the person with whom he is speaking, showing a hint of a smile. When this bystander to history became one of the main characters in the *Southern Weekly* incident, he had the advantage of years of careful observation and reflection. In particular, his reflections on the 1989 democracy movement and other historical social movements contributed to his ability to perceptively judge the situation at crucial moments.

Not without a hint of regret, Chen Mingyang noted that the 1989 pro-democracy movement ended in bloodshed rather than compromise, and that afterward the authorities greatly expanded economic freedoms while implementing ever-more-restrictive ideological controls. In the *Southern Weekly* affair, he and other core decision makers drew upon the lessons of the 1989 movement, ensuring that they left the Party a way out without it losing face. Chen also had nothing but praise for his younger colleagues at *Southern Weekly*, affirming their generally reasonable approach to this situation: "They all had an opportunity to become heroes, to be remembered by history."

14

GAME OVER

Newspapers in the Southern Media Group refused to carry the *Global Times* editorial, and no attempts were made to apply further pressure. Even as public outrage rose, the meeting everyone expected never took place.

In a separate WeChat group with members of the *Southern Weekly* news team, Cao Junwu had said that they might try a covert strike: not openly going on strike—but just not sending reporters out on the job.

News of such proposals quickly reached the managerial ranks, and Yang Xingfeng, Jiang Yiping, and Chen Mingyang all stepped forward to warn that any strike would do irreparable damage to the paper.

On the afternoon of January 8, several core staff members began discussing what sort of content they would include in the next edition of the newspaper. One thing of which they could be certain was that the provincial propaganda authorities would not get involved in this issue directly; they were taking a more hands-off approach for the moment. But as the discussion proceeded, it became clear that the censors didn't actually need to get involved—they were already inside the heads of *Southern Weekly* staff, whose self-censorship was reaching ludicrous new heights.

Shi Zhe had a draft of an article on hand about the recent public criticisms of the state's media monopoly. But in the end, even he voted it down. "It's probably not suitable to publish right now," he said.

Yuan Lei noted that the editors from the cultural desk had a series of pieces about war reporters and their stories during the war with Vietnam. Someone pointed out that veterans can be a sensitive topic. Yuan Lei countered that the reporters interviewed for the series were all from state media, and in any case similar stories had been published elsewhere already. But in the end, this topic was vetoed as well.

Yuan Lei joked bitterly: "Well then, why don't we just go ahead and start syndicating *Global Times* editorials?"

Xiang Yang and Yuan Lei then suggested another topic: a profile of members of the Nobel Prize Committee. But then again, the Nobel Prize had become a sensitive topic since the committee had awarded the Nobel Peace Prize to dissident intellectual Liu Xiaobo in 2010. At the prize ceremony in December 2010, an empty chair had been left for Liu, who was serving a prison sentence simply for his exercise of the constitutionally guaranteed right of free speech. For a moment in late 2010, the Central Propaganda Department had considered "chair" to be a sensitive term; a report on the Nobel Prize Committee was thus highly unlikely to be published, even today.

As the discussion proceeded, several people chain-smoked as though their lives depended on it, ignoring the "No Smoking" sign. Chen Mingyang fiddled as usual with his distinctive metallic cigarette filter. Rolling up a napkin, he wiped the corners of his mouth and proceeded to offer a basic principle to govern the next issue: "Let's not give them the impression that if they give us an inch of leeway, we go and try to take a mile."

The most important topic of discussion that day was how best to respond to the *Global Times* editorial in a way that would uphold *Southern Weekly*'s values. The group decided to run a piece called "What Kind of Newspaper is *Southern Weekly*?" in the "Ark Commentary" column, one of the paper's most respected regular features. The commentary would narrate the paper's history and its central role in China's reform and opening process. It would talk about the paper's focus on issues of concern to ordinary people in China. Cao Junwu wanted to title the piece "Born in 1984," but many staffers were opposed. The night before the paper went to press, the title was finally changed to "Establishing Our Stance as We Approach Thirty." The title was a reference to Confucius's description of his own learning as only attaining a systematic pattern and thus clear stance in his thirties: reading this title, you can have a sense of how self-satisfied and indeed overconfident the authors were in their attempt to "take a stand."

Inside the WeChat group, one side started to gain the upper hand on two core issues: whether to publish the next issue, and how exactly to respond to the broad support they had received.

Yuan Lei: Publishing this issue doesn't necessarily mean we're just giving in.

Shui Yin: I agree with Yuan Lei. We must publish. This is our responsibility, no matter the circumstances. If we don't publish the issue, things will only escalate. The result might be disastrous.

Huang Pu: I think we should publish information on Tuo Zhen's control tactics, offering an explanation to readers. We can make clear once and for all that this isn't just about the New Year's edition.

Yuan Lei: If everyone thinks this is our bargaining chip, then we should use that bargaining chip where it really counts, not just use it to provide an "explanation."

Tong Jiheng: I'm sorry but let me dump a bit of cold water on this suggestion: sharing that kind of information in our paper would be nothing short of suicidal. . . . Offering an explanation? To whom do we owe an explanation? And if we do provide an explanation, so what? Are they going to step back? Or suddenly disband the Central Propaganda Department?

Xi Di: I agree it would be suicidal. Party control of the media is the reality. Do we have evidence to show that Tuo Zhen's methods of control are uniquely crude? For the Party, that would just prove that he was doing his job! Second, aren't all those propaganda restrictions designated state secrets? Leaking state secrets is a criminal offense. Third, if we do go public, we are basically declaring war on the entire censorship system. That won't end well for us.

Tong Jiheng: We've already publicly announced the number of articles blocked or altered in 2012: 1,034. And in our statement, we made clear just how constraining we find these restrictions. We've already scored a moral victory. People sympathize with us. Do we really want to start some type of insurrection?

Shuang Qiao: Why is everyone getting so worked up? Our readers have given us such strong support. They don't want us to just stop publishing.

Yuan Lei: It would be really easy right now to make ourselves into either heroes or martyrs. It will be considerably more difficult to think through how to actually resolve the problems we are facing. And at a deeper level, what does "resolve the problems we are facing" even mean?

On the night of January 9, staff hurried to and fro. Preparation for the next issue was in its final stages, and an eerie yet anxious quiet hung over the newspaper's offices.

Around 9:30 p.m., Chen Mingyang and Zhu Hongjun, both members of the editorial board, appeared in the hall with a few colleagues. They were still talking about how exactly the "Ark Commentary" piece should be placed. Chen Mingyang hoped to place it on the front page, but a manager was opposed.

"They can't even step back and let us handle our own layouts," Chen Mingyang said unhappily. "Let's fight it. Let's fight it all. . . . I think we're in for a fight tonight."

Chen Mingyang's plan to resist evaporated just minutes later, when Wu Xiaofeng informed them that the column had been cut altogether.

Chen Mingyang had thought through all possible options. The best-case scenario would be running the "Ark Commentary" along with ten or more letters from readers. The next-best scenario would be running the commentary along with four or five readers' letters. Wu Xiaofeng piped up: "So what is the worst-case scenario?" Chen Mingyang responded: "My bottom line would be just running three letters from readers." Together, they thought through how they might argue their case.

Someone else chimed in, asking what they would do if none of the above scenarios proved possible. Even then, they said, they still must get the paper out.

Meanwhile, at a simple restaurant not far from *Southern Weekly*'s Beijing bureau, staff in the capital gathered once again. Deng Ke had just returned from Guangzhou. He urged everyone to ponder whether they should threaten to withhold publication of the next issue as a bargaining chip. Everyone shared their thoughts, and opinions seemed roughly evenly split. But then they heard the news of Chen Mingyang's various best- and worst-case scenarios, rendering the debate that they had just held meaningless.

Fang Kecheng says he will never forget the stale air that hung over their gathering that night. "When we heard what they were planning back at the head office, we were very, very confused. If this was their best-case scenario, well, there was no chance of any concessions."

Later, I had the chance to speak in detail with a few staffers about their views on what happened that night. A sampling of their comments is featured below.

Yang Jibin: "If we published the paper, we were suckers, but if we didn't, we were assholes. The newspaper was the only voice we had and whatever happened we still had to make ourselves heard."

Ju Jing: "I was in favor of publishing the next issue. It wasn't practical to continue resisting. The broader public support just wasn't there. *Southern Weekly* simply wasn't strong enough."

Chen Mingyang: "We decided internally to keep our expectations low. We didn't want a second 1989. All we really wanted was a different management style at our paper: nothing more, nothing less. How this played out in society had nothing to do with us. Speaking for myself at least, I'm not going to be a martyr for an impossible cause."

Qin Xuan: "From the standpoint of strategy, the only way to minimize risk for all of us was if this became a broader social movement. . . . But if our only concern was preserving the interests of a small group of writers and editors at *Southern Weekly*, there was no chance of a broader movement."

Among the paper's editors and reporters, there were numerous different trains of thought. Those who had recently joined, generally more eager and optimistic, suffered less under the daily regime of controls and as a result tended to take a more accepting attitude compared to hardened veterans. There were also regional differences. More than half of the reporters at the Beijing bureau tended to take more "radical" positions, while a majority at the headquarters in Guangzhou showed more restraint.

One by one, from Chen Mingyang to Shi Zhe to Cao Junwu to others, management warned of serious repercussions if the next issue did not go to press on time. The editors couldn't decipher whether management was actually insistent on this matter, or if they subconsciously just wanted to believe this to be the case, to take the easy way out.

With the looming threat of potential "major repercussions," the editors abandoned any attempts to even make a statement in the upcoming issue. Chen Mingyang decided it would be best if they simply avoided the controversy altogether, not even running correction notices concerning the New Year's special issue. Taking the path of least resistance, nothing would change.

Yang Jiwu made one last-ditch effort to resist. "If the commentary does not run," he said, "I'll refuse to sign off on the issue." Su Yongtong called him into Chen Mingyang's office, and Wu Xiaofeng hurried in as well. Chen's office was quite spacious, but he generally kept his L-shaped desk in the corner, wedging himself into the tiny space in the back. Chen explained his view of the situation—we've been tossed into the grinder, and while they're playing the long game, we are over here fighting over minute details. In the end, Yang Jiwu agreed to proceed as if nothing had happened. Game over.

For days on end *Southern Weekly* journalists found themselves torn between their desire for freedom and their desire for security. Security had now clearly won.

There was in the end no fierce internal struggle about the final decision to publish the next issue. Most staff members went along, having reached a point of near complete exhaustion. At one point, Cao Junwu grumbled: "After this, we just need to divide our tasks and get them done. Going on like this will ruin us." Su Yongtong knew that almost nothing could get between Cao Junwu and a good night's sleep, but those few days he had hardly slept at all.

Su Yongtong was exhausted as well. He would only go home and sleep for a bit, he said, after he had finished writing something. Then the phone would ring, and he would learn that some new problem had appeared. In the end, he found that he was unable to keep track of exactly how and when everything had unfolded. "With some of these matters," he said, "I'm actually unclear about what happened on which day."

Although everyone had been ground down by Tuo Zhen for at least half a year, and by Huang Can for even longer, after this week-long ride, most people felt that they had vented their grievances almost to the point of exhausting them. One week later, Su Yongtong would say that if there were any need to mobilize again, he feared he would not even have the energy.

Add to this the gradual feeling of helplessness and hopelessness as they were surrounded and enclosed on all sides, along with the faint fear that things could after all be even worse if they pushed back, along with their unwavering commitment to keeping this paper alive, even in a corrupted form—and that night, on the eve of publishing their next issue, imperfect as it was, an eerie and lasting silence finally descended over *Southern Weekly*.

15

GOING OUR SEPARATE WAYS

On the evening of January 10, Shi Zhe, the head of *Southern Weekly*'s reporting desk, flew to Beijing. As his flight descended through a dense layer of smog into the capital, he glanced out and saw something in the sky resembling a light gray wheel—this must be the sun, he thought, as seen from Beijing. His mission in the capital was to convince the paper's journalists there that the decision to go ahead with the latest issue was the right one. Their meeting at a high-end restaurant near the Guomao section of town went on for four hours, but at the end many of the journalists present still felt that the head office was surrendering far too easily.

Shi Zhe divided *Southern Weekly* staff into two main camps, one that he called the "self-preservation school" and the other the "social movement school." In reality, the division was not always so clear. Those who actually hoped for a larger social movement directly challenging the system were so few as to be negligible. The vast majority endorsed at least some type of resistance and were at the same time prepared to accept compromise. The real difference of opinion, however, concerned the nature and extent of such compromise. While some believed it would be victory enough if the newspaper could return to normal publication without overbearing restrictions, others believed this would waste an important ace card—withholding publication of the next issue in an attempt to force out Tuo Zhen or Huang Can. If both men remained in their positions and there were no promises of substantive change, nothing at all would have been achieved after all of this and everyone would eventually come to regret missing this opportunity. Some who wanted to apply more pressure to push out Tuo and Huang even felt that a triumphant last stand for *Southern Weekly* would in fact be far more meaningful than a continued compromised existence.

Fan Chenggang acknowledged that there were some policies with which he disagreed deeply. But in order to avoid damaging the paper's interests, he kept silent. Qin Xuan said that he was able to understand the decision to proceed with the next issue, because *Southern Weekly* could not and should not be the driving force in a social movement. Most contributors decided to keep their opinions to themselves.

Inside a WeChat group that brought together the more radically minded journalists at *Southern Weekly*, a few discussed their own internal conflicts:

Xiwan: In the general WeChat group, I can sense the true oppressive terror of what is commonly known as "public opinion."

Nonglin Xia: There is no escaping selfishness, slavishness, self-satisfaction, and foolishness. These too are part of human nature.

Hai Yue: I've been very critical throughout this whole process, because I feel that I should speak up sincerely about how I feel, even if doing so has almost no impact. But right now, what we need to do is heal this wound that is pulling us apart. No matter what anyone says, we need to keep the community intact—regardless of whether it's for *Southern Weekly* or for the future.

The task of explaining the end of this struggle was left to the group known as the "Frontal Command" and continued as the next issue went to press. On the morning of January 10, Chen Mingyang had sent a notification to some of his colleagues at *Southern Weekly*. Cao Junwu later shared the text on WeChat:

We tried, and we failed. This has been a genuine tragicomedy. And you all know that there is not much else that we could have hoped for. History will attest to this fact! But we must hold back both our laughter and our tears. Maybe sometimes not doing something is better than doing something. I beseech you to tell your colleagues, let's not take to the internet; let's not resign; let's not delay or strike. Let's go back to our jobs as reporters and editors. At least if we control or minimize issues of this sort, then perhaps in the end we can rewrite history. Of course, I might be too wrapped up in all of this at this point, losing sight of reality. But please, for the time being, trust in me!

No one commented. It was as though a flame had suddenly been extinguished.

Soon discussion in the WeChat group returned to the concerns of everyday life. An editor who lived in Guangzhou asked, "Does anyone want to head over to the newspaper offices with me for a swim later?" Another editor responded: "It's so frigid today, the cold will pop your belly button." Others pondered going out to play basketball or getting a bite to eat.

Shen Yachuan, a journalist for another Chinese paper, shared a post from a netizen supporter:

> This is what I've believed all along. That when this thing happened you all needed to have concrete and clear goals. When people came out to your door to support you, the least you could have done is have a representative come out to express your thanks and urge them to go home. Once things settled down, you could have made your own stance clear to the public. From beginning to end, however, there was nothing. There was nothing laudable in your response. In the future, I won't be working with the literati in the fight for democracy. It's best to leave you all to your writing.

Chang Ping, a former *Southern Weekly* columnist currently living in exile in Germany, also openly voiced his disappointment with his former paper: "If *Southern Weekly* has reached some type of an agreement with the propaganda department, then they need to explain this to everyone. They can't call for truth and transparency, then sneak into a dark corner to strike deals with this regime."

Jia Jia, a well-respected journalist, provided his own analysis of the situation: staff at *Southern Weekly*, he felt, had grown too accustomed to working inside the system. Even the most politically radical staff at *Southern Weekly*, he commented, were reformists, not real revolutionaries. Jia Jia said he couldn't really understand the overly cautious approach taken. If *Southern Weekly* views itself as a commercialized media outlet, he said, then they should treat their readers with more respect. Unfortunately, though, they never took the time to build up a real relationship with their readers and supporters. They were far too busy, he said, castrating themselves.

Gradually, people began to recognize that at the end of the day *Southern Weekly* belonged to the Chinese Communist Party and no one else. Attempting to overthrow the system from within the system leaves you no ground to stand on.

As both the *Beijing News* and *Southern Weekly* returned to their regular publishing schedules, online public opinion quieted down as well. As things suddenly settled, former *Southern Metropolis Daily* editor Liu Tianzhao shut down her laptop and decided she never wanted to hear about this matter again. For days, she said, she had practically forgotten to shower and sleep. As soon as she opened her eyes in the morning, she would hurry in what she called "a disheveled state" to do whatever she could to support *Southern Weekly*, from dawn to dusk. Like Chang Ping, the way things ended left a sour taste in Liu's mouth. She was even a little angry, feeling abandoned by people whom she had thought were allies.

But not everyone who supported *Southern Weekly* was disappointed. After Liu Yimu and the other protestors traveling with him returned to Changsha, they were again interrogated by local police. Despite the price they paid, they told me they understood and sympathized with *Southern Weekly*'s compromise. Du Ting, of the Hong Kong–based NGO Co-China, said that there was nothing she hated more than media control in China, but that at the end of the day everyone's health and well-being needed to be the priority.

In cities across China, from Beijing, to Shanghai, Hangzhou, Guangzhou, and beyond, vocal supporters of *Southern Weekly* were "invited to tea," a euphemism for informal interrogations with the Public Security Bureau. Weibo celebrities such as Kai-fu Lee and Ren Zhiqiang also received warnings.

After offering several days of heartfelt support for the paper, Taiwanese singer Annie Yi (Yi Neng Ching) faced official backlash. She lost her role as a judge on a popular reality show on Shanghai's Dragon Satellite Television and was blocked from holding concerts in China.

"When I saw people who had supported us being targeted, I sort of wanted to cry," said Su Yongtong. "This was one thing we did not do well. We should have spoken to them and made sure they wouldn't be in any danger." Staffers, he said, had been too cautious. "Many who supported us now despise us. I don't blame them. If I were one of them, I would hate us too."

Cao Junwu recalls that they had originally arranged to gather the various messages of support they had received from scholars and celebrities and respond to them one by one. But in the end, it just didn't happen. "From start to finish it just wasn't an organized movement. There was no strategy, and no core."

About six months after all this, I invited several firsthand observers to look back on the night that the flames feeding this incident suddenly died down. Deng Ke said he felt conflicted. He admitted that they had made the rational choice, but he also couldn't help but regret such rationality. After all, an alternate possibility had been lost to history. Fang Kecheng joked that all they had really done was talk big. He blamed the decision makers for their excessive conservatism. But at the same time, he realized that he might feel this way solely because he was so far from the center of the storm.

Fan Chenggang said that after the incident Cao Junwu urged them on numerous occasions to do the best that they possibly could in their reporting, because to do anything less would disappoint their supporters. Fan, however, still regrets that they did not do more to actually connect with their supporters. He told me that *Southern Weekly* staff did not articulate their values clearly to supporters, and that if they had only tried, they could have found a safe way to do so.

Looking back on this incident, Cao Junwu says that he doesn't feel there is anything he could have done to really change the situation. "If someone who can't swim suddenly falls into the rapids, what can they do but flail around?" he says. "With the benefit of hindsight, I suppose I could have flailed around a bit more gracefully."

A bit more gracefully—one approach that Cao Junwu really wishes they had pursued—was demanding that Huang Can resign on the day that the next issue was ready to go to press. It could have been done, he says. "The way we went about it all showed a real lack of knowledge about how to carry out this type of struggle. You don't really know what it's like until you're in the middle of it, and then it is impossible to find a path out."

Shi Zhe, a student of international politics, told me that anyone forced into a standoff with this regime will naturally be lost in fear. He regrets that they didn't even try withholding publication in order to demand concessions. Shi Zhe feels that they should have learned from the example of Taiwan's Democratic Progressive Party, whose fight for civil rights had transformed Taiwanese politics. Despite these regrets, he added, "We already made history."

The Thursday after the New Year's special edition, another issue of *Southern Weekly* hit the stands. The circulation department believed that this issue would sell well. They ordered larger runs in printing houses across the country, printing double the usual amount. It was only when Yang Haibin, the head of the circulation department, called local distributors that they realized how short-lived interest truly was. Distributors were eager to know why they had printed so many copies.

Circulation of the first issue back on the stands fell far short of expectations. At the newsstand closest to Southern Media headquarters, on the morning of January 10, the stack of newly printed papers stood a half meter tall. Six days later at least half remained, unsold.

16

THE AFTERMATH

Every year, *Southern Weekly*'s annual retreat is held in the middle of January. And so, as usual, in 2013 four large air-conditioned buses conveyed staff from the paper's headquarters in the center of Guangzhou to a luxury hotel on the edge of the city. According to tradition, staffers' first meal upon arrival was at a low-key country-style restaurant, where they enjoyed an oily meal of local freshwater fish. For many journalists at the newspaper, posted across the country, this was their one opportunity each year to get together with colleagues. But with everything that had just happened that month, the overall atmosphere at the gathering this year was a bit awkward. The opening dinner, in fact, ended abruptly, after just half an hour.

Nevertheless, the pomp and circumstance of the annual retreat remained unchanged. The hosts were careful to ensure that no one from outside the organization slipped into the retreat. There was one man waiting outside the restroom door to one side of the conference venue, and as soon as he saw anyone approaching the restroom, he would follow him or her with a list of questions. It turned out that he was an international journalist hoping for a scoop. He eventually left empty-handed.

Some had hoped the retreat could provide another opportunity to push Huang Can out. But Huang still sat at the main table, and he continued to preside over the gathering as the master of ceremonies. In their celebratory remarks, senior management avoided any reference to the recent controversy, like a festering wound no one wanted to touch.

During the typically predictable awards ceremony, there was one surprise. Generally, one award was given for the best unpublished news report. But this time, three awards were given for unpublished news reports. One editor told me that the managers handing out these awards reminded him of executioners comforting their victims with a fleeting moment of praise.

A meeting of the news department was held in a nearby conference room. Just as the discussion turned to the rumor that Huang Can would not be leaving his post as editor in chief, in stepped Huang with the rest of the senior managers. Would they continue to suffer under his rule? For many of the journalists present, even the thought was unbearable. As the meeting went on, criticisms of Huang came from all directions, while journalists privately strategized on WeChat about how they might force him out. By force of habit, Huang Can gripped his chin in his hand and swung his right leg as everyone spoke. When it came time for Huang to speak, he focused his comments on his successes as editor in chief. In the WeChat group, meanwhile, listeners vented their fury. "That whore," said one post. "Burn him with the tip of your cigarette," said another.

At the second day's banquet, Zeng Li, hoping to avoid becoming the center of attention, sat with the bus drivers at a table in the corner. Despite his best efforts, editors and reporters still sought him out and raised their glasses, toasting him. Before long, a line had formed before his table, not unlike the lines that had once formed at his door as reporters waited to debate cuts.

By midnight that night, the manager of the lobby bar had lost his temper at the chaos unfolding before his eyes, as the staff of the country's once-leading newspaper descended into drunkenness and tears. Aside from the drama at the hotel bar, the annual retreat came and went without any real news.

Just three months later, the General Office of the Chinese Communist Party issued Document No. 9 (officially titled "Communique on the Current State of the Ideological Sphere"), whose strident denunciations of democracy and constitutionalism as ruses intended to overthrow the Chinese Communist Party implicitly had *Southern Weekly* in its crosshairs. Initially, this document was passed along only internally to cadres and was not shared openly. Yet its distribution from the highest levels of the Party hierarchy signaled an intensification of the intellectual climate in China to a point that hadn't been seen since the dark years immediately after 1989.

At the end of March, Zeng Li received notice that the newspaper group would no longer employ retired cadres as news examiners. As the last puff of smoke curled up from his mouth toward the ceiling of his office, he felt an almost inexpressible sadness. He posted the following on his Weibo account:

> Today I walk away and become a free man. But in fact, freedom is nothing more than a dream. Nowhere on this earth are there truly free people, and certainly not in China. For decades now I've worked inside the system. I've followed the organization loyally. In neither speech nor action have I dared to step out of line. Only as retirement comes have I dared to utter a few words of what's truly in my heart. I'm leaving for good now, like the old saying, "after a long period of confinement, one returns to nature." I hope that even greater freedom may come. I dream.

Zeng Li hoped to do a grand tour of North America. He wanted to see the "civilized world," he said. Tragically, after just five days of freedom, on the night of April 3, Zeng enjoyed a few drinks during a family dinner before suddenly suffering a gastrointestinal hemorrhage. He was rushed to the hospital but passed away the next day.

Editors and reporters at *Southern Weekly* were shocked by Zeng Li's sudden passing. But aside from attending his formal memorial service, they were prohibited from organizing any other public commemorations. And they didn't even try to resist, as Zeng once had; it was as though they had been caged. Many were all too aware of their own glaring cowardice. One journalist felt as though they had all left the better part of themselves behind with Zeng Li.

Huang Can attended Zeng Li's memorial service. He made a deep and affected bow, and then stood there for a moment in silence.

By the middle of January, Huang Can had again begun wielding his red pen over the paper's proofs. He seemed to go at it with greater gusto than ever before, exercising ever tighter control over already rigorously controlled content. Often, the editors would just turn a blind eye to his changes, choosing instead to go around Huang and seek the advice of Wang Genghui, who had a reputation as a somewhat more open-minded censor.

Huang Can, however, was determined to exercise his power as editor in chief as fully as possible. When the time came for the group to assign university graduates to various media within the organization, Huang Can went out of his way to ensure that the personnel department did not hire anyone involved in the protests.

The paper's editorial committee continued to have limited influence. As the first half of 2013 came to an end, a journalist in the Shanghai bureau of *Southern Weekly* voiced his displeasure on an internal group chat: "At the annual retreat, there was an excited attempt to establish a better governance model for the paper, supposedly enhancing collective leadership in order to limit the powers of the editor in chief. What a joke! How many empty promises have we fallen for?"

On the bright side, the prepublication censorship system had ended, and Tuo Zhen seldom showed his face around the office.

At the end of May, Yang Jian was transferred to Hong Kong, where he became deputy head of the Liaison Office of the Central People's Government. This is an important position in which Yang could expect to deal with a much freer media as well as more wide-scale oversight and even opposition from the public.

Tuo Zhen and Huang Can, the men who provoked trouble through their "loyalty" to the Party's media management system, were never held accountable for the events of early 2013. In August, Huang Can was promoted to chairman of *Southern Weekly*'s newspaper group. There was no longer any need for him to involve himself in the details of the proofing process and the many potential controversies that inevitably arose in this process.

As Huang Can continued to rise in the ranks, Chen Mingyang was removed from his position. This change was generally interpreted as a move by the propaganda authorities against major players in the events of early January. Soon thereafter, Cao Junwu and Yang Jibin quit. On the form that he was required to fill out to make his departure official, Yang provided a memorable explanation: "I no longer love this job."

As this chain reaction continued to unfold, Ye Weimin and a number of other younger reporters also decided to leave *Southern Weekly*. Reflecting on these departures, Cao Junwu commented, "It's like after an earthquake, you can't see on the surface, but the internal structure of the mountain has been forever changed. Just one rock rolling out of place can generate a landslide."

One night in Panyu, after a light rain had blown through, Cao Junwu chose another natural metaphor to think through these events. "The storm will return," he says, "and when it does come, I'll be prepared. That, more than anything, is what I've taken away from this experience."

Cao Junwu, Shi Zhe, and the others have all envisioned their "next time." But as for when that next time will come, and what it might look like, no one can really say.

INDEX

ABOUT THE AUTHOR AND THE TRANSLATOR

Guan Jun is a former *Southern Weekly* journalist and writer. He is the author of *Footprints* (2013), a study of the impact of the 2008 Beijing Olympics on China, and *The Greatest Offense against Filiality* (2012), a discussion of the author's decision not to have children.

Kevin Carrico is senior lecturer in Chinese studies at Monash University. He is the author of *The Great Han: Race, Nationalism, and Tradition in China Today* (2017) and the translator of Tsering Woeser's *Tibet on Fire: Self-Immolations against Chinese Rule* (2016).